C000132228

'In keeping with his previous p[...] latest volume is a biblical-the[...] laboriously working through th[...] Christian debate concerning [...] this topic within its broader b[...] fully demonstrating how the prospect of rest with God finds its eschatological fulfilment. Readers are thus helped to think carefully about the topic in a biblically-informed manner. This stimulating and pastorally encouraging discussion will surely enrich the spiritual lives of us all.'

Paul Williamson, lecturer in Old Testament,
Hebrew and Aramaic, Moore Theological College, Sydney

'Graeme Goldsworthy applies a lifetime of in-depth scholarships to the current existential sense of spiritual "homelessness", reflecting along the way with the themes of the exile from Eden and the unhelpful and helpful ways of considering "the city". He deftly guides the reader to think biblically about the notion of rest and the Sabbath. The result is an accessible, beautifully written book that focuses on Christ and the writings of his apostles, all within a sensible overall theological framework.'

Paul Barnett, Lecturer Emeritus,
Moore Theological College, Sydney

'What is your life's goal? In this concise, clear, and convincing book Graeme Goldsworthy explores this fundamental question through a masterful interweaving of three biblical themes. To bring the storylines of exile, the city, and sabbath together is novel, but within a framework of biblical theology the exercise proves to be rewarding. I enthusiastically commend this book, which can be enjoyed by novice and expert alike.'

Andrew Shead, Head of Department of Old Testament
and Hebrew, Moore Theological College, Sydney

Good news for the people of God

Homeward Bound

Sabbath rest for the people of God

Graeme Goldsworthy

Paternoster:
thinking faith

First published 2019 by Paternoster
Paternoster is an imprint of Authentic Media Ltd
PO Box 6326, Bletchley, Milton Keynes MK1 9GG.
authenticmedia.co.uk

British Library Cataloguing in Publication Data
A catalogue record for this book is available from the British Library

ISBN 978-1-78893-027-7
978-1-78893-028-4 (e-book)

Cover design by Arnel Gregorio
arrowdesigns01@gmail.com

Printed and bound by CPI Group (UK) Ltd, Croydon, CR0 4YY

So then, there remains a Sabbath rest for the people of God, for whoever has entered God's rest has also rested from his works as God did from his.

Heb. 4:9–10

Contents

Dedicated to the memory of
Donald William Bradley Robinson (1922–2018)
Vice Principal, Moore Theological College 1959–73
Archbishop of Sydney 1982–93

Preface

How the Old Testament and its diverse themes relate to the Christian is something most of us either struggle with or simply put in the too-hard basket. Yet, we must engage this task if only because Jesus and his apostles regarded the Old Testament as a book about the Christ. Furthermore, until the New Testament books were written and accepted, the Old Testament contained the only Scriptures the first Christians had to nourish their faith in Jesus. Christianity is a historic faith in that it is based on the unfolding history of salvation contained in the Bible. Because of this progression in God's revelation, different parts of the Bible connect in different ways to the Christian's life in this twenty-first century. The biblical examination of any topic involves us in the need to understand how the revelation of the Bible is structured. I want to promote such understanding through this study.

The approach to the Bible as a unified collection of sixty-six books in order to understand both its unity and diversity is what the discipline of biblical theology is about. In this study I refer to 'biblical theology' several times. It is a term which means more than a theology that is biblical, as against an un-biblical theology; it is about the revelation of God in the Bible as it progressively unfolds and finds its climax in the person of Jesus. The themes I have chosen all come from the book of Genesis and are closely linked through the history of the emerging nation of Israel. Their convergence and amalgamation in the person and work of Jesus are then applied to us who are in union with Christ by faith in his person and work. Because the Old Testament is ultimately a book about Christ, it is fundamental to the faith of all of us who are in Christ and are defined by our relationship to him.

It is a matter of great satisfaction to me personally to have Paternoster publish this work. It was Paternoster that published my first three studies in biblical theology.[1] It is a pleasure and a privilege to have this work also in their care. I am grateful to the staff at Paternoster, especially for Becky Fawcett's oversight, the editorship of Mollie Barker, and all who have worked to make this publication possible. On the home front, my grateful thanks go to my wife Miriam who, over our fifty-four years together, has always been an encouragement and patient supporter as I spend hours researching and writing. Above all, I thank God my Father for giving me the time and ability in my senior years to continue this ministry of writing about his gospel of grace in Jesus our Lord and Saviour.

Graeme Goldsworthy
Brisbane

---

[1] *Gospel and Kingdom* (1981), *The Gospel in Revelation* (1984) and *Gospel and Wisdom* (1987). The three are now published as a single volume, *The Goldsworthy Trilogy* (2000).

1

Introduction: Which Day of Rest, and What May I Do on It?

When Christians consider what is appropriate as a Sunday activity, the 'elephant in the room' is often the Sabbath law and what it should mean to us. The fourth of the Ten Commandments will be familiar to most Christians; and it is one that generates a certain amount of controversy among us:

> Remember the Sabbath day, to keep it holy. Six days you shall labour, and do all your work, but the seventh day is a Sabbath to the LORD your God. On it you shall not do any work, you, or your son, or your daughter, your male servant, or your female servant, or your livestock, or the sojourner who is within your gates. For in six days the LORD made heaven and earth, the sea, and all that is in them, and rested the seventh day. Therefore the LORD blessed the Sabbath day and made it holy.
>
> *Exod. 20:8–11*

Soon after I graduated from theological college and was ordained to the Anglican ministry in Sydney, a fellow student of mine was waiting for a train at Central Railway Station. It was early on a Sunday morning, and he was dressed in a suit with clerical collar, and on his way to parish duties at a suburban church. An older man approached him and said: 'Excuse me, sir. What day is the Sabbath?' He was almost certainly a Seventh-day Adventist out to convince the young curate of his Sunday-Sabbath errors. But, without hesitation, his quarry answered, 'Saturday.' Apparently, his adversary was so surprised to get the very answer that he had never expected that he simply walked away in confusion. Yet, that subject remains today as one area of controversy for us: which day *is* the Sabbath, and how should we spend it? For many Christians, not Saturday, but Sunday, the Lord's Day, has become the Christian Sabbath. There are differences in the manner of observance since Christ has come, but Sunday is still regarded as the Sabbath.

In my student days, I was for a while a member of a small local orchestral ensemble. We were preparing for some special occasion and agreed to meet on a Sunday afternoon for rehearsal at the home of one of the players. Rehearsal finished; cup of coffee consumed; and then our hostess asked: 'Anyone like to hit a tennis ball?' So, there I was on her tennis court happily hitting a ball around with others when the horrible truth struck me: it's Sunday! Now, I had been brought up on the explicit, and the implied, 1950s values of Sydney Anglican evangelicalism. No one had ever told me: 'It's OK to play music on Sunday, but not to play tennis.' Yet somehow, I had formed that conviction. Over the years my thinking has developed and changed somewhat, especially as I learned about the discipline of biblical theology as a fruitful way of examining such issues.

Before I ever got to study at Moore College for the Anglican ministry, I was especially concerned to understand how Old Testament passages applied to us as Christians. I used to puzzle over the recital of the Ten Commandments in the Communion Service in the (1662) Book of Common Prayer (BCP). The congregational response to each commandment is 'Lord, have mercy upon us, and incline our hearts to keep this law.' I often wondered about what it meant to keep the Sabbath law. Was it simply to make Sunday special? I had no problem with that: the normal pattern for me was Sunday school or Bible class, followed by Morning Prayer. Some respite in the early afternoon, then off to Youth Fellowship, followed by Evening Prayer, and probably to someone's home after church for coffee. Not much time or opportunity to work and break the Sabbath!

During my theological studies, I was introduced to the formal discipline of biblical theology. It soon became clear to me that this approach to Bible study is not a concern reserved for ivory-tower academics. Rather, it is something all Christians should be concerned with. It deals with the implications of the unity of the Bible and how the various parts relate to one another. It focuses on the theology (God's revelation) of the Bible in the way it comes to us in the Bible. Especially, it is concerned with how the Old Testament relates to the New Testament. I had read in my denomination's confession of faith, the Thirty-nine Articles of Religion (1562), the words of Article VII, *Of the Old Testament:* 'The Old Testament is not contrary to the New: for both in the Old and New Testament everlasting life is offered to Mankind by Christ, who is the only Mediator between God and Man, being both God and Man.' I discovered that the 'big picture' contained in the Bible as a unified whole meant that there was a certain dynamic and historical development to biblical revelation. Thus, the progressive nature of revelation within history tells us that not all parts of the Bible have the same relationship to the Christian believer. Every Christian, not just the professional academic, is faced constantly with questions of how the Old Testament testifies to Christ as the one mediator between God and human beings.

All Christians, including our children, need to be taught to come to terms with the nature of this unity of the Bible, a unity summed up in Christ.[1]

This study of the Sabbath rest is intended as a contribution to our appreciation of the biblical theme of 'rest', and how this theme should impinge upon our understanding of faith and life. We all need to learn how to deal with the fact that the entire Bible consists of the one word of God, about the one way of salvation through the one Saviour Christ. In this study, I will consider the central theme of the Sabbath rest, along with some related themes that help us to assess the meaning of that central theme for twenty-first-century Christians. While it is easy to say that the early church adopted Sunday, the Lord's Day, as its Sabbath, a biblical-theological study of the themes I have chosen in this investigation suggests that the truth is not only more complex than that simple solution but also much more edifying for our Christian living.

---

[1] My first published treatment of biblical theology is *Gospel and Kingdom* (Exeter: Paternoster, 1981), now part of *The Goldsworthy Trilogy* (Milton Keynes: Paternoster, 2000). A more detailed discussion can be found in my book, *Christ-Centred Biblical Theology: Hermeneutical Foundations and Principles* (Nottingham/Downers Grove, IL: Apollos, 2012).

2

Rest: Belonging Somewhere and Getting There

*You have made us for yourself, O Lord, and our
heart is restless until it rests in you.*
                    Augustine of Hippo, Confessions, Bk I

The subtitle of this book, *Sabbath Rest for the People of God*, may
appear to indicate a consideration of how Christians should
spend Sunday. The usual treatment for such an approach is to
specify that Christians should not work, but instead should
meet, worship and rest on Sunday. End of story! Of course,
there is usually no argument that we should acknowledge
Sunday as the Lord's Day. There also ought to be no argument
that Christians need to meet regularly for worship, teaching and
fellowship. But in fact the Sabbath rest is a lot more interesting
and complex than merely having rules or customs for Sunday.
Rest is an important biblical theme that goes way beyond Israel
being commanded to stop work one day in seven.

Relationships and Meaning

Humans are sociable beings; most people feel the need to belong somewhere and to connect with other people. The recluse,

on the other hand, is often seen as abnormal, weird, and a hater of self and others. A sense of belonging is what holds together our social structures, whether it is the family, a sporting club, a church fellowship, or the idea of neighbourhood. And that is before we get to the obvious matter of national pride.

Relationships provide the grounds for attributing meaning to our existence. Without a sense of meaning we are restless. The creation account in Genesis 1 defines human beings by relationships. There is no attempt to define us physiologically, psychologically, or sociologically. We are created in the image (Hebrew: *tselem*) and likeness (Hebrew: *d^emut*) of God, and those two words are used to describe our relationship to God.[1] In Genesis 1 and 2 we are defined in terms of relationships, first to God, and then to other people, and finally to the created order. We find our true humanity by going outside ourselves towards God and other people, and by rightly relating to the whole creation. This is the very opposite of mystical religions and existential philosophies which encourage one to go inwards to find oneself. These philosophies define us by what

---

[1] These two words, found in Genesis 1:26, are generally taken by commentators as an example of *hendiadys*, two words to indicate one and the same thing. The image of God is a relational term. However, the second-century theologian Irenaeus declared that image and likeness mean different qualities in humankind. In time, this distinction became the theological position of Thomas Aquinas, who did so much to shape medieval Roman Catholicism. He established firmly the distinction that said the *image* is our natural property as humans, and the *likeness* is the supernatural added grace that makes for eternal life. Luther rejected this distinction and rendered the passage 'God said, let us make man, an image that is like us' (translation mine). Much hangs on these different views, but that is another story!

is supposed to be inside us. The Bible defines us by relations to who and what is outside us. In this way, being created in God's image means that we somehow reflect the divine society: the relationship of the three 'persons', Father, Son and Holy Spirit, within the unity of the one God.

Genesis also describes the human relationship to the remainder of creation as one of having dominion over it. Humans express this dominion by intellectual endeavour, scientific research and technological achievement. Agriculture, animal husbandry and benign environmental control also express this dominion. Architecture and the arts likewise come under this mandate. The overall hierarchy of relationships is quite simply presented: God rules absolutely, and humans, being in his image, are deputized to rule the remainder of the creation. As God rules for our good, so we are called on to rule creation for its good. But, in our broken world, relationships break down or we move apart, and even the most sociable person can experience intense loneliness. In fact, the more sociable a person is, the more intensely loneliness will be experienced. The dominion, referred to in Genesis 1:28, is corrupted to become the self-interested quest for power, domination and exploitation. We will need to consider further how the most socially and relationally oriented person, Jesus of Nazareth, suffered the loneliness of the cross on our behalf. We observe something of this in his cry of dereliction from the cross: 'My God, my God, why have you forsaken me?' (Mark 15:34).

The Journey of Life towards Inevitable Death

When we turn to the questions of belonging, relationships are again to the fore. And belonging usually implies some place we can call home. In addition to human relationships, linked with our idea of home are our needs of rest and recuperation, leisure-time and recreation. We know the body and the mind both need times of relaxation and rest. We simply cannot carry on working without let-up. We grow weary, and we have learned that regular time off from work to sleep or to do some 'non-work' activity is needed. We learn that we need to sleep for a certain number of hours each day and that we need some time off in a week.

In societies with a Judeo-Christian background, we may well have been taught that a weekly rest-day is linked with the biblical account of creation and the idea of a Sabbath rest. The seven-day week and the one day off in seven both stem from the Old Testament's command to refrain from work on the seventh day. Most Christians don't mind changing this to the first day of the week. Since we cannot put a precise date on day one, we cannot know when the actual seventh day is. We are thus content to make it one day in seven. Many Christians hold the conviction that Sunday, the first day of the week and the day of Christ's resurrection, has taken over as the Christian Sabbath. In our affluent society, for most people it has become the whole weekend that we all take off from work. Nevertheless, the erosion of the Christian Sunday through sport or Sunday trading is a concern for us and, inevitably, the question of the Sabbath commandment arises. Is there a Christian Sabbath, and how should it be observed?

We can see from these few thoughts that two ideas are closely linked: home and rest. Both are concerned with relationships. But we also know that our present concerns go further than simply where we live and how long we work. There are questions of how many hours in the day we work, and what day or days are given to us as time off from work. Assuming we stay fully employed, we work until we reach a certain age and then retire. We live longer on average than people of past generations, and thus many delay the final stage of life which is our death. But should we regard our death as our leaving home, or as our going home?

Most people understand the initials RIP even if they don't comprehend the original Latin words for which they stand.[2] The English translation '[May he or she] rest in peace' reminds us of the notion of death being a rest. Christians commonly think of dying also as 'going home to be with the Lord'. The expectation is the restoration of perfect relationships for eternity. Atheists and many others entertain no such hope of a life after death. They will assert that death is the end, and oblivion is all we can anticipate as 'rest'. They reject the biblical notion that we have a relationship with God because he created us. So, death means we simply cease to be; there are no more worries and no further labour; only nothingness. There are also many popular, but quite unbiblical, variations on the idea that the dead are consciously somewhere else; even 'looking down on us'. Others will assert that we 'live on in the hearts of those we leave behind'. This may or may not be good news for those we do leave behind, but it hardly advances our own personal and self-conscious prospects! Most of us would like to be well thought of even after we are gone. But for Christians who take seriously the words of the Nicene Creed: 'I look for the resurrection of the body and the life of the world to come', there is the clear inference that we leave home to go home. So, although we look for times of rest during this life, and although we have a concept of home as our shelter and a place to rest, as Christians we expect to be fully self-aware in our final going home to an eternal rest, whatever that may turn out to be like.

It has become somewhat of a cliché to refer to our life as a journey, but it is not without logic. Movement through time

---

[2] *Requiescat in pace.*

and space means change, which most people hope will be a change for the better even if we do not relish the prospect of old age. Many English-speaking Christians of my generation have probably sung, especially at funerals, James Montgomery's hymn 'Forever with the Lord'.

> 'Forever with the Lord!'
> Amen, so let it be!
> Life from His death is in that word,
> 'Tis immortality.
> Here in the body pent,
> Absent from Him I roam,
> Yet nightly pitch my moving tent
> A day's march nearer home.[3]

Going home and being at rest are closely related. When we speak of a Christian who has died as having 'gone home to be with the Lord', we think of this home as the place of eternal rest. Yet we would not think of that rest as an endless 'shut-eye'.

In this study, I examine some connected biblical themes which all relate to the journey of life and the aspirations we have for 'going to glory'. A while ago a friend of mine, who like me has reached senior years, commented to me: 'When we finally get to glory, we will really wonder why we spent so much time and effort trying to stay out of it!' But that is what we do, and rightly so. We look forward to being with the Lord, but not before we have a long and fulfilling life in the here and now. After all, God has put us here for a reason. Nevertheless, there is a universal quest for rest. I intend to examine the following themes related to the ultimate biblical idea of rest:

---

[3]   James Montgomery, 1835.

- Exile and homelessness: humanity's expulsion from God-given rest
- The city as humankind's first futile attempt to find rest without God
- The Sabbath rest: its definition and the promise of God-given rest
- The authentic Christian life of rest while still moving towards our rest.

One obvious reason for embarking on this kind of study relates to our present life. If we are not yet in our real and desired home, how should we esteem the life we have during our allotted time on earth? What should be our attitude to the planet we live on now? How do we deal with the ambiguity of being in this world but belonging to another realm: the kingdom of God? Paul remarks that 'our citizenship is in heaven' (Phil. 3:20). He urges us to 'put to death therefore what is earthly in you' (Col. 3:5). But a popular saying raises for us the question: is it possible to become so heavenly minded that we are of no earthly use? I trust this study will point us to some answers to these questions.

A Biblical Theology of What?

Recently I was asked to write an article on 'Home' for a Christian journal.[4] The only guidance I was given was that it should be a biblically based consideration of the theme. So, how does

---

4   Graeme Goldsworthy, 'A Day's March Nearer Home', *CASE* [the quarterly magazine of the Centre for Apologetic Scholarship and Education at New College, University of New South Wales] 38 (2014): pp. 4–9.

one deal with a theme that, on the surface, has many nuances in the biblical story? A concordance was not much help.[5] The words 'house' and 'home', meaning the place we live, are found quite frequently in the biblical literature. And when they do occur, it is mostly in the context of a narrative text. I suspect, however, that there is a difference between a place to spend the night and a home; the reason is relationships and a sense of belonging. Furthermore, there is certainly a difference between even an ideal earthly home, and the hope of an eternal home and rest in the presence of our Lord.

Once we engage in a little lateral thinking we find ourselves with a growing list of biblical ideas that are interconnected by their relationship to the central story of the Bible. The difficulty with this arises from the nature of the Bible as an organic unity but with much diversity. This means that we must limit the number of themes we consider or the whole exercise will simply get out of hand. *The unity of the Bible means that every part of it has some connection with every other part.*[6] That is why I have tried to select biblical ideas that are most central to the theme, and which have clear connections with one another. What does the Bible say about 'home' and 'rest'? I have chosen to look at the central theme of humankind's journey from the Garden of Eden towards the final consummation of the kingdom of God. Somewhere in that is the individual journey that each one of us is presently making. Also linked with it

---

[5] For the uninitiated: a concordance is a comprehensive volume that lists alphabetically all the words occurring in a specific version of the Bible (KJV; NIV etc.) and references in biblical order all the places in that version where these words are found.

[6] One of the practical purposes of biblical theology is to help us discern the real and important connections between the various parts of the Bible.

are the above-mentioned themes that emerge from the biblical account of humans outside Eden, and the narrative of the way God has acted to restore a people to himself in his kingdom.

I intend this to be a non-technical (layperson's) biblical-theological approach to the chosen central theme. While there are various ways to engage in such a study, my chosen method of a biblical-theological study of any theme or themes involves looking at them in relation to three discernible stages in God's revelation.[7]

The first stage is the biblical history of the Old Testament, and especially the period of the covenant people from Abraham to Solomon's dedication of the temple. The entire Old Testament history is relevant, but the period from Abraham to Solomon is especially significant. In it, the covenant is given its first expression in the promises to Abraham, and then reaches its climax with Solomon.

The second stage of revelation overlaps the first. It involves the prophetic promises of the future coming of the kingdom on what some prophets refer to as the Day of the Lord.[8] During this stage, in the period after Solomon, Israel's experience of home and rest comes to be radically disrupted. It is corrupted internally through idolatry and apostasy, and externally by incursions of foreign invaders. The prophets declare God's indictment of the sin of Israel and Judah, and they pronounce his judgment that will surely come to pass. But the prophets also have words of comfort and assurance because of the faithfulness

---

[7] I first expounded this general approach in *Gospel and Kingdom*, and have explained it in detail in my book *Christ-Centred Biblical Theology: Hermeneutical Foundations and Principles* (Nottingham/ Downers Grove, IL: Apollos, 2012).

[8] For example: Isa. 2:12; 13:9; 34:8; Jer. 46:10; Ezek. 13:5; 30:3; Amos 5:18; Zeph. 1:8,18; 2:2,3; Mal. 4:5.

of God to save. The coming judgment will involve the destruction of all the earthly and tangible evidences of God's covenant: the people's place in the promised land; God's city, Jerusalem; the temple; and the Davidic kingship. Nevertheless, the prophets proclaim that the Day of the Lord is coming.[9] This day will bring in the fullness of God's kingdom, accompanied by final salvation for God's faithful people, and final judgment for the enemies of his kingdom. These predictions remain unfulfilled in the Old Testament period.

The third stage of revelation comes with Jesus Christ who is declared to be the fulfiller of the prophetic promises. We will find much about the subjects of 'home' and 'rest' in the ministry of Jesus. It is important that we allow God's final and fullest word of revelation, the New Testament testimony to Jesus as Saviour and Lord, to provide the definitive interpretation of all that foreshadows him and his kingdom in the Old Testament. Thus, stage one examines the biblical history, and especially that from Abraham to Solomon. Stage two is concerned with prophetic eschatology.[10] Stage three looks at what it means for Christ to be the fulfiller of all God's promises.

When it comes to considering how Jesus Christ fulfils the Old Testament themes, we need to take account of the New Testament's distinctions between first, the perfect and finished work of Christ (the gospel event); second, the not yet finished, nor yet perfected work of the word and Spirit within believers and the world; and third, the anticipated

---

[9] Note that 'Day of the Lord' is simply a Hebraic way of saying 'the Lord's Day'.

[10] Eschatology (Greek: *eschatos*, last) is a broad term referring to the future as it is progressively revealed by God, the consequent future hopes of God's people, and their fulfilment.

consummation of Christ's work when he returns in glory to judge the living and the dead. To preach the gospel is to proclaim the incarnate person and the earthly ministry of Christ. It concerns the once-for-all, perfect and finished saving work of Christ. The gospel is what we must believe if we are to be saved. Since the gospel is the proclamation of the perfect and *finished* work of Christ, the history of the gospel event begins with conception of Jesus in the womb of Mary and ends with his ascension to the right hand of the Father on high to send the Holy Spirit on his people. It may also be said to include the message of Jesus that he will one day return to consummate his gospel.[11]

Only by observing these distinctions can we deal with the tension within Christian existence between who and what we are as justified sinners, and what will be the final consummation of the gospel. The gospel concerns the work of Jesus to do for us what we could not do for ourselves. Since it is the completed and perfect work of Christ on the grounds of which we are justified by faith, this has implications for our assurance of salvation, and for the way we live. It also has significant ramifications for our understanding of the biblical idea of 'rest'. We should be precise in understanding the difference between what God did *for us* in Jesus, and what the Spirit of God goes on doing *in and through us* as a result.

---

[11] While the second coming of Jesus is not part of the gospel event, Jesus' teaching that he will return is something we must believe. The second coming is a prime implication of the gospel event, and it was an important part of the apostolic proclamation. However, it is important to understand that we are justified by faith in what Jesus has done, not by believing what will transpire when he returns.

Thus, in addition to the three overall stages of revelation, we recognize three aspects of Jesus' work within the third stage of our biblical revelation (fulfilment in Christ). These are:

1. What God did *for* us in Christ (the gospel);
2. What God goes on doing *in* us by his word and Spirit (the fruit or effects of the gospel);
3. What God will one day do along *with* us when Jesus returns in glory to judge the living and the dead (the consummation of the gospel).

When we consider our themes of home and rest we see that they are implicated in different ways by these three aspects of God's work. We should also remember that these important distinctions never imply separation: it is all the one work of God.

I want to leave us with some sense of the present application of the matters investigated. There is also the motivation of our desire to reach the final goal of glory that God's word sets out for us. We need to develop a biblically based perspective on where we have come from, what our present status is in Christ, and what is the final goal towards which we move. These factors should affect the way we think about our present life, home, family life and our hope for the future. In the final analysis, the Sabbath rest is a biblical notion governed by the nature of the gospel and how it bears fruit in our lives.

In Search of the Biblical Idea of the Sabbath Rest

Although my chosen themes are all connected, it may not be obvious on first sight how they relate in explaining the central theme of the Sabbath rest. In this chapter I set out to survey briefly the chosen themes so that their interconnectedness will be more apparent.

i. Exile and homelessness: humanity's expulsion from God-given rest

The Sabbath rest points to the situation that needs to be resolved by such a rest. There is a radical sense of unrest in our lives that cries out for resolution. The biblical narrative highlights the chosen people in exile moving as pilgrims towards a home with God. We can trace that theme through the three stages mentioned above. The problem of exile is never resolved in the Old Testament, although the prophets have much to say about a future coming of final salvation as a resolution of Israel's exile. Then, in the New Testament, we find that Christians are likewise seen as aliens in this world and on a pilgrimage towards the goal of God's kingdom. This speaks of a radical homelessness that is universal and far more comprehensive than the lack of somewhere to sleep and to take shelter from the elements.

The biblical story tells of the first human pair at home in the Garden of Eden. But the narrative takes a sudden and unpleasant turn: Adam and Eve rebel against God's authority, and their rebellion leads to their expulsion from that home. This is commonly referred to as 'the fall', but we can easily become desensitized to the seriousness of what is described in Genesis 3. For all of us, our present existence outside Eden is the only life we know. Many will experience this life as one of hardship, poverty, broken families and homelessness. But many of us will experience it as life in reasonable comfort and affluence in a world that is still beautiful and enthralling. Even the daily delivery by various news channels of horrors somewhere else on our planet does not necessarily disturb our complacency. For the secular mind, humanity's common problems, which Christians assign to the fall, can all be fixed by therapy, education, full employment, better housing, stronger measures for law and order, or all the above. We may even acknowledge that we are imperfect beings in an imperfect world. But we will never be able to really understand the full disaster of the fall until the Holy Spirit opens our minds to understand what God needed to do to fix it! It took the incarnation of God the Son, God becoming man, and the suffering and death of Jesus, to restore people to God. That shows us how bad the problem really is. The entire biblical narrative from Genesis 3 to Revelation 20 tells of the plan and purpose of God to restore a people to himself in his kingdom. Biblically speaking, humanity leaves home and its true rest in Genesis 3, and does not return home until a redeemed remnant finds the rest described in Revelation 21 and 22.

ii. The city: humankind's first futile attempt to find rest without God

This may seem to be a theme that is rather remote from the central theme of the Sabbath rest. I include it because the city is presented in a surprising way very early in the biblical story as humankind's first attempt to find rest without God. Urbanization is a global phenomenon and it carries with it all kinds of problems. Many people may still entertain the idea of an ideal pastoral life in the country. These are usually the ones who are tired of traffic jams, noise, crime and air pollution.

However, the global trend is quite the opposite as rural populations flock to the cities to escape hunger, unemployment, drought, fire and floods, and to find higher education and jobs. It is there also that culture, the arts and higher education are concentrated alongside all the seamier aspects of urban life. We are dependent on our cities. Thus, it is pertinent to our enquiries that the city figures so prominently in the biblical story. If Eden or paradise is the original ideal of home, the biblical account comes to link a unique city with it, so that the final vision of John's Apocalypse is that of the heavenly Jerusalem. This celestial city in Revelation 21 is connected to the new Eden portrayed in Revelation 22. But before we get to the disclosure of this city of God, another city, Babylon the Harlot, must be destroyed. I suspect many, perhaps most, Christians envisage heaven as a kind of rural paradise.[12] There is no doubt that images of a return to Eden persist throughout the biblical story. Yet the final vision is of the heavenly Jerusalem combined with the life-giving features of Eden.

iii. The Sabbath rest: its definition and the promise of God-given rest

When we turn our attention to God resting on the seventh day after his creation of the heavens and the earth, the biblical narrative inevitably draws us to consider the meaning of the Sabbath. There are other 'rests' that occur in the biblical story that relate to the people of God entering the promised land. The significance of the Sabbath in the Old Testament comes

---

[12] The name 'Paradise' is derived from a Persian word that means a garden or orchard.

to be linked with Israel's entering such a rest. We must ponder if there is ongoing meaning for Christians of the Sabbath law of Israel. How the law of the Sabbath does or does not apply to us today is a matter concerning which there are different views among Christians. The risk of touching on a subject that generates some controversy should not deter us from trying to understand it.[13]

iv. The authentic Christian life of rest while still moving towards our rest

Home, as the place where we dwell, is not a prominent theme in the Bible if we search for it under that name. There are, of course, plenty of references in the narratives to people's homes. But in this study, I want to concentrate on the home as the life-goal we all have; the destination towards which we travel. This pilgrimage is motivated in part by the sense in which we are not yet there.[14] Integral with our Christian faith is the acceptance of the universal human condition of homelessness. Now, homelessness, as the plight of many people even in affluent western societies, is something we rightly regard as a social evil that must be addressed. We should never try to play down the plight of the homeless in our cities and towns.

---

[13] While the Articles of Religion are silent on the matter, the Book of Common Prayer (1662) includes the rehearsing of the Ten Commandments in the Service of Holy Communion. The Westminster Confession (1646), chapter XXI, is entitled 'Of Religious Worship and the Sabbath Day'.

[14] Perhaps we may suggest that there is a theological reason that explains why our children, a few minutes into a half-day journey, ask, 'Are we there yet?'

Even in our increasingly secularized western societies, homelessness is now seen as a major social problem for our politicians and charities to address. Nevertheless, the Bible teaches us that, until we achieve the final goal, there is a sense in which we are all lacking a true home. Comfortable affluence in modern living easily obscures the reality that we, as dwellers outside Eden, are still homeless. We may need to remind ourselves that we live in a world in which things are not as they should be. We also recognize that the Christian message is one of hope that one day things will be, finally and for ever, exactly as they should be. Remember that the word *hope* in the Bible refers, not to a mere wish that something perhaps might eventuate, but to a firm conviction based on God's promises of what certainly will be. Moreover, the way things should be, and will be, is defined by the plan and purpose of God through his Son.

We Begin with Where We Are Now

I suspect that many of us find the study of the Old Testament an exercise in navigating through unfamiliar and difficult terrain. That is why I prefer to begin where we are as Christians, and in the part of the Bible that is most familiar to us. I intend, first of all, to probe the New Testament, and particularly the four gospels, for some clues to the themes under investigation, and how these themes are related to the person of Jesus and to the gospel events. While doing this, we will find many references, both explicit and implicit, to the background to these themes in the Old Testament. One thing the study of the New Testament constantly confronts us with is the way the authors interpret the Old Testament in the light of

Jesus Christ.[15] A thematic study will, of necessity, investigate
the antecedents to the New Testament in the Old Testament.
By antecedents I refer not only to some general background
material but, more specifically, to the identifiable theological
themes that are developed in the Old Testament and brought
to their fullness in the New Testament. Another way of looking
at this relationship between the Old Testament and the gospel
is that the template, the structure, of the gospel event has its
foundations and development in the Old Testament.[16] That is
why Christians can make such statements as the one quoted
above from the Thirty-nine Articles.[17] When we tackle matters
in this way, we not only start in familiar territory, but we also
learn from the outset how the Old Testament foreshadows the
New Testament and finds fulfilment in it. In each of my chosen
themes I will begin with Jesus in his gospel. I will then return
to the Old Testament to examine the background to the New
Testament's treatment. I will finish with a consideration of the
implications for us now as those who are in faith union with
Christ. Christ is our Alpha and Omega, the first and the last;
thus, we start with Christ that we might end with Christ.

---

[15] A comprehensive study of this is found in *Commentary on the
New Testament Use of the Old Testament* (ed. G.K. Beale and D.A.
Carson; Grand Rapids, MI: Baker/Nottingham: Apollos, 2007).
For a concise, simpler, and non-technical, treatment see my
book, *Jesus through the Old Testament* (Abingdon: Bible Reading
Fellowship, 2017).

[16] For example, note Paul's statement that the gospel of God was 'promised beforehand through his prophets in the holy Scriptures' (Rom.
1:2). Also, 'And the Scripture, foreseeing that God would justify
the Gentiles by faith, preached the gospel beforehand to Abraham,
saying, "In you shall all the nations be blessed"' (Gal. 3:8).

[17] See above, p. 3.

3

Exile and Homelessness: Humanity's Expulsion from God-given Rest

Charles Wesley's now famous and very popular hymn 'And Can It Be' speaks of the incarnation of God the Son thus (verse 3):

> He left his Father's throne above,
> So free, so infinite His grace,
> Emptied himself of all but love,
> And bled for Adam's helpless race:
> 'Tis mercy all, immense and free;
> For, O my God, it found out me!

Clearly, if we are to sing this verse with understanding, we must allow Wesley some poetic licence in suggesting that the Christ 'emptied himself of all but love'. Taken literally, this line gives little indication of Christ's glorious deity united with his humanity in his coming to earth. But Wesley clearly believed in the full deity of Jesus.[1] The point of his words here is that

---

[1] So: 'Amazing love! How can it be/That thou, my God, shouldst die for me?' (verse 1, 'And Can It Be') or 'Veiled in flesh the Godhead see;/Hail, the incarnate Deity' (verse 2, 'Hark, the Herald Angels Sing').

God the Son left home to come among us as a servant. We are in exile now and, as a species, we have been in exile since Adam and Eve were expelled from Eden. The amazing truth of the incarnation is that God, in Christ, joined us in our exile.

Home and Homelessness: God in Our Exile

The incarnation, in a very real sense, meant that God the Son left home as he came into a fallen and hostile world. The alienation of the creation from the Creator, because of human sin, meant that for God to take on human flesh in this world was a self-imposed sharing of our exile from Eden. It was not that God's own original creation could have been an alien world to him, for in Eden God is spoken of as walking in the garden in the cool of the day (Gen. 3:8). But in the incarnation God came anew to share the plight of sinful human beings who have been cast out of Eden into a fallen world, having become a species at enmity with God. God enters the sphere of his own judgment on sin. Although he was God, God the Son took the form of a servant and became obedient even unto death (Phil. 2:5–8). The subsequent exaltation of Jesus, his resurrection and ascension, was a return to his rightful place of honour with the Father (Phil. 2:9–10). It was the acceptance of true humanity, the perfect humanity of Jesus, into the presence of God the Father. Since then, we have had a man in heaven on our behalf. Thus, Paul's claim that Jesus was 'raised for our justification' (Rom. 4:25) indicates that the resurrection of Jesus was the demonstration that God the Father accepted him as the one human being who is worthy of a place in the divine presence. To be that, he needed to live, suffer and die on our behalf. As our representative, Jesus is now the grounds of our justification and full acceptance with the Father.

The homelessness of Jesus of Nazareth is consistent with this fact of the divine submission to exile. In the four gospels, Jesus is almost never spoken of in connection to a home to which he can go and rest. He begins his earthly life as one born in a stable among the animals (Luke 2:6–7,16). One of the few references to his being in a house is when the wise men visit him as an infant (Matt. 2:11).[2] Nowhere do we find anything that approaches a description of what we would regard as normal home-life for Jesus. If it did exist the gospels do not remark on it. He is identified as Joseph's son (Luke 4:22) but there is no description of Jesus at home with Joseph. There is hearsay evidence given that he spent time at home as a carpenter with his father. This may be true, but the direct evidence is not there.[3] Of course, if he didn't begin his ministry until he was thirty, he must surely have been occupied with something in the meanwhile. Also, Joseph fades out of the picture early in the narratives and ceases to be of interest to the narrators.[4] Anything that ties Jesus to a normal home-life is muted.

The gospel accounts tell of Jesus as constantly on the move, a process that began when he was an infant and had to be taken to Egypt to escape Herod's wrath (Matt. 2:13–15). Matthew gives us a clue here, for he tells us that the return to Judah

---

[2] The common idea that the wise men are present at the birth of Jesus and worship the infant alongside the shepherds does not sit with the biblical evidence. Placing them in our Christmas nativity crib is understandable but inaccurate.

[3] In Matt. 13:55, Jesus is identified as the carpenter's son; and in Mark 6:3, probably the same event as in Luke 4:22, the question is posed: 'Is not this the carpenter?' But we are not told directly that he was.

[4] Outside the infancy narratives Jesus is identified as Joseph's son in Luke 4:22 when he speaks in the synagogue at Nazareth, and in John 6:42 after he fed the five thousand. Apart from those occasions Joseph is not mentioned again.

fulfilled Hosea's reference to Israel's exodus from Egypt (Hos. 11:1).[5] In this way Matthew indicates that he understands Jesus as the true Israel of the exodus. Egypt was a place of exile for both Israel and Jesus. Israel's goal was the promised land of Canaan and, in an important sense, this was home. But the glory of Israel under David and Solomon was transitory. And even the promised land was never a new Eden.

Not only does the 'exile' of Jesus fulfil the role of Israel's exile, but it also recalls Isaiah's description of the return from the Babylonian exile as the Lord being with them and himself returning from that exile on the way prepared for him:

A voice cries:
'In the wilderness prepare the way of the LORD;
    make straight in the desert a highway for our God.'

Isa. 40:3

Fear not, for I have redeemed you;
    I have called you by name, you are mine.
When you pass through the waters, I will be with you;
    and through the rivers, they shall not overwhelm you . . .

Isa. 43:1–2

Fear not, for I am with you;
    I will bring your offspring from the east,
    and from the west I will gather you.

Isa. 43:5

---

[5] Hosea makes a historical reference to Israel's escape from Egypt. As such it is not a prophetic prediction or promise. Matthew apparently understands Jesus as the true Israel coming out of Egypt and thus as fulfilling Hosea's statement.

Isaiah thus foreshadows the coming of the Lord as one in which he is intimately involved in the exile of his people, and in their return from it. It is significant that Luke's account of Jesus in the temple, and his apparent disconnectedness from his earthly home (Luke 2:41–52), is followed by Luke's interpretation of John the Baptist as fulfilling Isaiah's prophecy of the Lord's exile (Luke 3:2–6, quoting Isaiah 40:3–5). Like Isaiah, both Jeremiah and Ezekiel had spoken words of comfort to the Jewish exiles in Babylon that reassured the people that God was with them even when they were removed from the promised land. For example: Jeremiah's vision of the two baskets of figs declares that the good figs represent the people who are in Babylon (Jer. 24:1–10). His letter to the exiles tells them to live a normal life until God should bring them home (Jer. 29:1–23). Ezekiel's restoration oracles are full of comfort for the exiles in Babylon (Ezek. 34 – 37).

Luke recounts the episode of the boy Jesus being found in the temple (Luke 2:41–52). After the customary Passover celebrations in Jerusalem, 12-year-old Jesus becomes separated from his parents. They eventually find him back in the city among the teachers:

> After three days they found him in the temple, sitting among the teachers, listening to them and asking them questions. And all who heard him were amazed at his understanding and his answers. And when his parents saw him, they were astonished. And his mother said to him, 'Son, why have you treated us so? Behold, your father and I have been searching for you in great distress.' And he said to them, 'Why were you looking for me? Did you not know that I must be in my Father's house?'

Luke 2:46–49

Jesus is found in the temple where he claims he belongs. He redirects the term 'father' away from Joseph to mean his heavenly Father whose house the temple is.[6] It is difficult for us to comprehend what it was like for Mary and Joseph to have the incarnate God as their child, but we do get a brief glimpse here. The incident shows that the boy Jesus was beginning to grasp the meaning of his own relationships and the reality of his homelessness in this world.

Thus, Jesus is portrayed as never having had any sense of arriving home while he was here on earth. His family's return from Egypt was met with uncertainty as the child was taken to Galilee and then Nazareth (Matt. 2:22–23). Matthew also refers to Jesus coming to his own city which is Capernaum, but there is no reference to home-life there (Matt. 9:1; see Matt. 4:13). The disciples of Jesus are portrayed as leaving their home-life as they knew it to follow him. In the New Testament, the references to disciples being followers of Jesus is almost exclusively confined to the time of the Lord's earthly ministry when following him was literally a matter of leaving their nets (Mark 1:18), leaving their father in the boat (Mark 1:20), or leaving the tax booth (Luke 5:27–28), and following him on the move. Thus, becoming a disciple of Jesus was often a matter of literally leaving home.[7] When a scribe tells Jesus that he is willing to follow him, the reply he receives is not encouraging: 'Foxes have holes, and birds of the air have nests, but the Son of Man has nowhere to lay his head' (Matt. 8:20). Being a follower of Jesus was for the disciples a matter of literally joining him in his ministry and in his homelessness.

---

[6] The Greek is literally 'in the things of my Father', but he was found in the temple doing temple things.

[7] The word 'disciple' (Greek: *mathētēs*) occurs only in the gospels and Acts. It is not used in the epistles to describe Christian believers.

Being a Christian, then, is rarely referred to in the New Testament epistles as 'following Jesus'; perhaps the closest to this is 1 Peter 2:21: 'because Christ also suffered for you, leaving you an example, so that you might follow in his steps.' To 'follow' is here a metaphorical reference to the imitation of the example left by Jesus. Paul describes a similar situation as having the same mind 'which is yours in Christ Jesus' (Phil. 2:5). John describes his apocalyptic vision of the 144,000 'who follow the Lamb wherever he goes' (Rev. 14:1–5). This also has the ring of a metaphorical description of the people of God. After the ascension of Jesus, being his follower is not the normal way the New Testament describes believers. This, however, does not diminish in any way the New Testament perspective on our present existence as being outside the desired home which is the kingdom of God.

It seems, then, that there is a fundamental reason why Jesus is portrayed more in terms of homelessness than in those of domesticity. When he enters houses to teach or perform some healing miracle, he is not entering his own house. He has come to deal with the human condition which has existed since our first parents were exiled from Eden. This means that we also are sojourners and exiles in the world until we arrive at the new Eden. For Jesus to be the saviour, he must deal with our homelessness by becoming homeless for us and with us in our world. It is the nature of the gospel that Jesus identifies with us in dealing with the ravages of our sin. Christians generally have some idea of Jesus dying on the cross in our place, as our substitute. But do we ever contemplate the evidence that the life of Jesus was also both representative and substitutionary? In short, he submitted to God's judgment in a life of homelessness from the kingdom, so that we might regain a home in God's kingdom.

The ultimate exile for Jesus was his death on the cross. It dealt with the sanction expressed in Genesis 2:17, 'for in the day that you eat of it you shall surely die.' That Adam and Eve did not immediately drop down dead when confronted by God after their disobedience does not mean that God had second thoughts and commuted the sentence to life imprisonment (Gen. 3:8–13). 'You shall surely die' is fulfilled in exile from Eden, in the disruption of the created order, and in the certainty of human mortality (Gen. 3:22–24; see Rom. 8:20–23).

While the gospels portray Jesus as an alien in this fallen world, his death is not the end. The exaltation of Jesus, his resurrection and ascension, is his homecoming; his return from exile. He comes to the Father after he has accomplished all that is necessary to save God's people and to inaugurate a new creation. His homecoming to the Father means the homecoming of all who are united to him by faith. His goal is expressed as his finished saving work in unity with his Father. The eternal life of his flock is consequently secure for ever: 'My sheep hear my voice, and I know them, and they follow me. I give them eternal life, and they will never perish, and no one will snatch them out of my hand. My Father, who has given them to me, is greater than all, and no one is able to snatch them out of the Father's hand. I and the Father are one' (John 10:27–30). Thus, when Jesus returns to the Father, he does not forsake his disciples who are left behind. After all, they are the Father's gift to him and are eternally safe in his hands. He goes to prepare a place for them (John 14:2–3). We learn that his home is our home and that our goal is to 'come to the Father'. The Father of Jesus becomes truly our Father: 'I am the way, and the truth, and the life. No one comes to the Father except through me' (John 14:6).

In the context of the promise to send the Holy Spirit (John 14:15–17), Jesus indicates that this means that he will be present with his disciples:

I will not leave you as orphans; I will come to you.

John 14:18

If anyone loves me, he will keep my word, and my Father will love him, and we will come to him and make our home with him.

John 14:23

In the latter passage, you will notice that home is where Jesus and the Father are, and there is a real sense in which we are not yet there.

So, where do we belong? What can we call home, and why? The gospels have only rather indirect ways of anchoring our existence in terms of our earthly dwellings. Jesus invites people to himself, but it is a two-edged sword. To be one of his disciples is to invite the hostility of the world. On the one hand, he says, 'Come to me, all who labour and are heavy laden, and I will give you rest' (Matt. 11:28). On the other hand, he warns, 'Do not think that I have come to bring peace to the earth. I have not come to bring peace, but a sword' (Matt. 10:34). And, 'In the world you will have tribulation. But take heart; I have overcome the world' (John 16:33). It does not appear that the disciples of Jesus really belonged here in this world which is hostile to the kingdom of God. Furthermore, Jesus promised his disciples that they would be with him even though he was going away from their presence: 'In my Father's house are many rooms. If it were not so, would I have told you that I go to prepare a place for you? And if I go and prepare a place for you,

I will come again and will take you to myself, that where I am you may be also' (John 14:2–3). Whatever we can say about our earthly homes, for the Christian the real home is where Jesus is, and our ultimate desire is to be with him.

Before we move on, a word is needed about the biblical use of the word 'house'. This word (Hebrew: *bayit*; Greek: *oikos*) is one of the most frequently used nouns in the Bible, occurring over 1,800 times. Furthermore, 'house' can mean either a dwelling or a dynasty (see 2 Sam. 7:10–13). It can be used to designate a household, a word that is usually focused on the people living in the house rather than upon the dwelling itself. It is also used to refer to the people of the nation as 'house of Israel'. It is important to grasp the specific nuances of the word in its various uses in different contexts. In today's real-estate terms, 'house' and 'home' convey little by way of personal relationships except as the potential for constructing a building as a place for family life. In the Bible, this is not often found. One important exception is the prescribed tabernacle, and then the Jerusalem temple, as a dwelling place for God in which his people find fellowship with him.

The Bible deals with the message of the God who has mercifully allowed the rebellious human race to survive even while under the ultimate sentence of death (Gen. 2:17). Graciously, he allows us to live in families and communities in which we build our shelters from the elements as safe places to live and to raise and nurture children. Overarching this earthly existence, which the secular mindset usually treats as our only home, is the plan of salvation that will bring the people of God to an eternal home and rest. Jesus comes to us where we are: into whatever communities and homes exist for us now. The gospel message shows that the universal instinct for another home that transcends our death is well founded. But it also emphasizes that the only way to it is through God's Christ. What, then, is the Old Testament background to this gospel message?

The Old Testament and Exile

The whole of the Old Testament narrative, from the time Adam and Eve were expelled from Eden to the end of the story of Israel, is about people in exile. The exile continues into the New Testament and is our present condition. Space permits only a brief survey of the human exile and homelessness.

Let me remind you again that 'house' and 'home' are not necessarily the same. The two overlap in our common usage and in the way the Bible uses them. The houses we live in, our city or our country are all in some degree 'home'. In general terms, home is where we belong. The story of humankind begins with our creation, and Genesis 1 describes the events of the sixth day of creation with the making of human beings:

> Then God said, 'Let us make man in our image, after our likeness. And let them have dominion over the fish of the sea and over the birds of the heavens and over the livestock and over all the earth and over every creeping thing that creeps on the earth.'
>
> So God created man in his own image,
>   in the image of God he created him;
>   male and female he created them.
>
> *Gen. 1:26–27*

The author describes what it means to be human in terms of relationship to God: humankind is made in God's image, after his likeness. God speaks to the humans and defines further their relationship to the rest of creation both animate and inanimate:

> And God blessed them. And God said to them, 'Be fruitful and multiply and fill the earth and subdue it and have dominion over the fish of the sea and over the birds of the heavens and over every living thing that moves on the earth.' And God said, 'Behold I have given you every plant yielding seed that is on the face of all the earth, and every tree with seed in its fruit. You shall have them for food. And to every beast of the earth and to every bird of the heavens and to everything that creeps on the earth, everything that has the breath of life, I have given every green plant for food.' And it was so. And God saw everything that he had made, and behold, it was very good.
>
> *Gen. 1:28–31a*

In this declaration, God is further describing his relationship to humankind. His sovereign decree not only designates where humans belong, but it tells us of what this belongingness consisted. If, in anticipation, we call this creation situation 'home', it is characterized by relationships that are clearly stated.

Human beings are not only created by a sovereign word from God, 'Let us make man in our image . . .', but are also defined by that sovereign word. The simple statement, 'And God blessed them', is most likely explained by what follows: the gifts of procreation and dominion, and the provision of all their needs. With this God is satisfied, for it is 'very good'. This is followed by the statement that God rested on the seventh day. We will return to this rest of God in chapter 5 of this book.

When we turn to the second creation account in Genesis 2 we find again that the key notion is relationships. First, we are told of the man's home: 'And the LORD God planted a garden in Eden, in the east, and there he put the man whom he had formed' (Gen. 2:8). Second, we are told of boundaries of the man's freedom which establish the principle of obedience to the word of God. This obedience is closely related to right thinking about reality: 'The LORD God commanded the man, saying, "You may surely eat of every tree of the garden, but of the tree of the knowledge of good and evil you shall not eat, for in the day that you eat of it you shall surely die"' (Gen. 2:16–17). Finally, we are told of the relationship of the man to the woman because, 'It is not good that the man should be alone' (Gen. 2:18). Adam rejoices in the woman as the appropriate helper for him:

> 'This at last is bone of my bones
> and flesh of my flesh;
> she shall be called Woman,
> because she was taken out of Man.'

Therefore a man shall leave his father and his mother and hold fast to his wife, and they shall become one flesh. And the man and his wife were both naked and were not ashamed.

Gen. 2:23–25

What is not mentioned is anything as ordinary as a shelter or house. Home is Eden where the human couple relate to God, to each other, and to the creation around them according to the words spoken to them by God the Lord. I have suggested elsewhere that God's people in God's place under God's rule are the essential aspects of what we later come to know of in

Scripture as the kingdom of God.[8] There is no other way to define 'home' other than relationally. Not only is there no mention of a domicile for the humans, there is also no house for God. Eden is the temple and home; the dwelling place of God with his people.

The sin of Adam and Eve, as recounted in Genesis 3, involves several relevant issues relating to the matter of knowledge and truth. The serpent's attack starts by casting doubt on the truthfulness of God's word: 'Did God actually say . . .?' (Gen. 3:1). Then he flatly contradicts God's word: 'You will not surely die' (Gen. 3:4). The humans succumb to the temptation, and in doing so they cease to think God's thoughts after him and act on the presumption that they can independently determine truth. The serpent thus succeeds in bringing about a radical realignment of human thought processes. Quite independently of God's word, they take it upon themselves the prerogative of God to judge what is true and what is not true. Then, the once perfect relationship of the man and his wife gives way to blame, self-justification and shame. Finally, we see the incompatibility of human rebellion and a home in the kingdom of God: the pair must leave the garden. The curses which are visited on the serpent and on the human pair reach their climax in the expulsion from the garden:

> The LORD God said, 'Behold, the man has become like one of us in knowing good and evil. Now, lest he reach out his hand and take also of the tree of life and eat, and live forever—' therefore the LORD God sent him out from the garden of Eden to work the ground from which he was taken. He drove out the man, and at the

---

[8] See my book *Gospel and Kingdom*, now published as part of *The Goldsworthy Trilogy* (Milton Keynes: Paternoster, 2000).

east of the garden of Eden he placed the cherubim and a flaming
sword that turned every way to guard the way to the tree of life.

Gen. 3:22–24

Outside Eden, humankind is homeless. Everything that made
for authentic human existence has been lost: fellowship with
God through his creating and ruling word; a right relationship
to other humans; and the mindset that allows God to define
created reality and our relationship to it. The fall, as we call it,
was not an inadvertent stumble over an unforeseen object, or
the peccadillo of eating a piece of fruit. It was, rather, a radical
and wilful moral revolt against the authority of God, the Lord
and Creator of heaven and earth.

The hint of a future redemption, which is found in the curse
on the serpent (Gen. 3:14–15), is the one bright element in
this depressing narrative. On the grounds of this prediction
we dare to look for the eventual homecoming of a redeemed
humanity. The other hopeful element is the fact that fallen existence in a fallen world is allowed to continue by God's grace.
Whatever else the threat of death in Genesis 2:17 signifies, our
final and inevitable death comes after a period of existence on
this planet. The ongoing predicament within this life is later
described by Paul as being 'dead in the trespasses and sins in
which you once walked' (Eph. 2:1–2,5).

But things must become worse, considerably worse, before
they get better. So, the story of Cain and Abel highlights the
moral lostness of humanity. Cain murders Abel and is driven
out from the 'home' that rebellious men and women have
devised. They are already outside Eden but have managed to
make a home of sorts in the fallen world. That is the way humanity has been ever since. 'Home' now is where fallen rebels
make it. We can only marvel at the grace of God that allows life

to continue after the rebellion of Adam and Eve. Why the decree 'you shall surely die' is not executed immediately and fully is given no direct answer in Scripture. One solution often proposed is that Adam and Eve died spiritually, not physically. The physical death is delayed, but it inevitably comes and we return to the dust. This solution does not really explain why humanity continues at all. The answer may not be explicit in Genesis 3:15, but it does emerge from this prediction. Not only the act of creation itself, but also every step in the process leading to redemption is of God's eternal purpose of grace. The light of God's grace begins to shine as it points us to the kingdom of God that has its prototype in Eden. In hindsight, we can say that God's eternal plan was to show his grace in the gospel. Only the gospel can explain why the sin of Adam did not result in the immediate and complete obliteration of the human pair along with the rest of creation.

To summarize: the exile of humanity begins with the ejection from Eden described in Genesis 3. The proto-evangel in Genesis 3:15, a foreshadowing of the gospel, prepares for the announcement of God's grace that will continue with the human race, and will eventually restore his people to the kingdom. Every expression of redemption from Genesis 3:15 onwards foreshadows the definitive act of redemption that Jesus effects by coming amongst us, sharing our exile, and dealing with the causes of it in humanity's rebellion against the Creator. Although the name Immanuel ('God with us') occurs as a name only three times in Scripture (Isa. 7:14; 8:8; and Matt. 1:23 which is a quotation of Isa. 7:14), the assurance that God is with his people is everywhere.[9] It comes in the

---

[9] Sometimes this assurance comes in the form of the simple Hebrew phrase *'immanu 'el* which translates literally as 'With us [is] God.'

form of promises, the covenants, and the prophetic assurances of salvation. Its substance lies in the saving acts of God that his ungrateful people experience throughout their history. The narrative of the people of God from Noah onwards is a story of the acts of God which, despite the many words of judgment on a wayward species, is a story of grace and salvation. It is a story of sovereign grace that conquers the human determination to be free of God's rule. It is the story of the Creator Lord who follows humankind into the homelessness of the wilderness to seek and to save the lost (Luke 19:10).

Our starting point in this chapter was to note that the incarnation is the coming of the God-Man to be our Immanuel, 'God with us'. Jesus as God in our exile brings to a climax a theme that goes back to the beginning. From the moment Adam and Eve are driven out of Eden, humanity is in exile. But God does not forsake us and, in that sense, he is prepared to go into our exile for the sake of his people and his kingdom. That God deals graciously with Adam and Eve, Abel, Seth and their line of descendants through Noah to Abraham, shows that he is involved with us here in our homelessness. Any biblical-theological study of 'grace' would need to include the creation, followed by the continuing favour of God towards rebellious humans. The mighty demonstration of his power to save Israel from its exile in Egypt is further proof of God's grace and presence in this fallen world. But it is not only the prophetic word of God concerning his actions to judge and to bless that show his involvement. We must reckon on the purposes of God that he is working out for the restoration of his people and the creation itself.

God is with his chosen people as he makes covenant with them. The promises to Abraham in Genesis 12:1–3 are reiterated in Genesis 15:1–6,18; 17:1–8; and 22:17–18. They are repeated to Isaac, Abraham's son, in Genesis 26:2–5,23–24. Then it is Jacob's turn to be reminded of the covenant in Genesis 28:3–4 and 28:10–17. In this latter passage, Jacob dreams of a ladder to heaven above which the Lord stands and confirms the covenant now with Jacob. In response Jacob expresses awe: "'Surely the LORD is in this place, and I did not know it." And he was afraid and said, "How awesome is this place! This is none other than the house of God, and this is the gate of heaven"' (Gen. 28:16–17). This is the first reference to a house of God. Jacob's placing a stone as a pillar that 'shall be God's house' may seem premature, even lacking in understanding. In the context, however, there is no reason to suppose that Jacob for one moment thinks God lived in this stone (Gen. 28:18–22). Jacob names the place Bethel, house of God. This is the gate of heaven, for even now the transcendence of God is perceived. The stone stands as a memorial to Jacob's experience of the presence of God and of the confirmation of his promises. It will become clearer from the law of Sinai that God's dwelling in the fallen world will be mediated through the tabernacle and its priestly ministry (Exod. 25 – 30). But, from the beginning, the people of God had to deal with the growing awareness of both the transcendence and the immanence of God. In this, they grasped at least the foreshadowing of the incarnation when the transcendent God became immanent in Christ.

When the Israelites are redeemed from the power of the Egyptians, they receive God's law through Moses at Sinai; a body of instruction concerning the redeemed life. Included in the law is the direction to build the tabernacle as God's dwelling, and to institute the ministry of the priesthood: 'And let them make me a sanctuary, that I may dwell in their midst. Exactly as I show you concerning the pattern of the tabernacle, and of all its furniture, so you shall make it' (Exod. 25:8–9).

It is an act of merciful condescension that God makes himself available in Israel's exile, and provides for ongoing reconciliation and fellowship with his redeemed people. This is shown by the ark of the covenant and the mercy seat that will express the presence of God in their midst:

> And you shall put the mercy seat on the top of the ark, and in the ark you shall put the testimony that I shall give you. There I will meet with you, and from above the mercy seat, from between the two cherubim that are on the ark of the testimony, I will speak with you about all that I will give you in commandment for the people of Israel.
>
> *Exod. 25:21–22*

It is difficult to avoid the implication that the cherubim guard the mercy seat, the symbol of the presence of God, in the way the return to Eden is guarded by the cherubim when Adam and Eve are driven out (Gen. 3:24).

However, the release from Egypt does not bring about a return to the purity of Eden. Even the entry into the promised land, and the subsequent possession of it, do not bring the full reality of the kingdom of God. The tabernacle and the declared presence of God in it show us two things about the relationship of Israel and the Lord: outside Eden God is graciously pleased to dwell among his people, but he does not keep open house. Sin continues as a barrier between God and his chosen people. While Adam and Eve once had a direct relationship with the Creator, now that relationship must be mediated through the priestly ministry involving sacrifice for sin. The tabernacle is fenced, and the ark of the covenant is housed in the Most Holy Place where none may enter except the high priest, and he only once a year (Lev. 16). However close the pious Israelite may have thought the presence of God to be, there is always the tangible reminder that the presence of God is one that is mediated graciously to a sinful people.

It becomes clear from the relevant narratives that Israel's stay in Canaan, though very different from the slavery of Egypt, is nevertheless not the fullness of blessing promised to Abraham. At best, even the glories of David's and Solomon's kingdoms are only a foreshadowing of the kingdom of God. 1 Chronicles records David's preparations for the building of the temple. As he dedicates the people's offerings he prays: 'But who am I, and what is my people, that we should be able thus to offer willingly? For all things come from you, and of your own have we given you. For we are strangers before you and sojourners, as all our fathers were. Our days on the earth are like a shadow, and there is no abiding' (1 Chr. 29:14–15). David has been anointed as the messiah-king, but he nevertheless understands this situation of exile in the context of the salvation history going back to Israel's ancestors. He knows they are but passing through. Sojourners, by definition, are not at rest: their stay is temporary.

Solomon's temple gave a more permanent expression of the dwelling of God in their midst than the tabernacle did. But even the glorious temple is destined for destruction. While the exodus from Egypt demonstrated the need for a redemptive miracle to bring God's people into the promised land, both aspects are but a foreshadowing of the reality yet to come. Even when they experience the glories of the kingdoms of David and Solomon, the Israelites inhabit only a shadow of the kingdom of God. As it continues to be with Christians, they are in the world but not of it; the faithful are of the kingdom of God while not yet in it. The lesson we must learn is that expressed by David: 'Our days on the earth are like a shadow.'

The Babylonian exile (sixth century BC), like the Egyptian exile before it, may seem to negate all the promises of God to the descendants of Abraham, Isaac and Jacob. Judah's exile from the land is accompanied by the destruction of every tangible expression of the promises of God in the land: the holy city Jerusalem, the temple, and the rule of the Davidic dynasty. Yet the faithfulness of God is proclaimed by the prophets. If Babylon is another exile from what is already an exile, God is nevertheless still with them. So, the Lord shows Jeremiah a vision of two baskets of figs; one full of good, choice fruit; the other full of rotten fruit:

> Thus says the LORD, the God of Israel: Like these good figs, so I will regard as good the exiles from Judah, whom I have sent away from this place to the land of the Chaldeans. I will set my eyes on them for good, and I will bring them back to this land. I will build them up, and not tear them down; I will plant them, and not uproot them. I will give them a heart to know that I am the LORD, and they shall be my people and I will be their God, for they shall return to me with their whole heart.
>
> *Jer. 24:5–7*[10]

Ezekiel describes visions of the glory of the Lord ascending from the Jerusalem temple, and then leaving the city (Ezek. 3:23; 9:3; 10:4,18–19; 11:23). As part of his extraordinary restoration oracles, he speaks of the glory of the Lord returning from the east to a renewed temple (Ezek. 43:1–5; 44:4). His final words are to describe the restored Jerusalem as the city named 'The LORD Is There' (Ezek. 48:35). Both these prophets

---

[10] The terminology here reflects the positive side of Jeremiah's commission in Jer. 1:10.

of the exile express the astonishing truth that God is pleased to accompany his people into this new exile so that in his own good time he might bring them back from exile to their land. But this return itself turns out to be only a shadow of the true exodus achieved through the messianic Son of David, Jesus of Nazareth, who came among us to share our exile and to lead us out of it.

The book of Daniel also tells the story of God's presence with his people in exile in Babylon. Daniel and his friends are plainly among those whom Jeremiah has described as good figs. Through them, the sovereignty of the God of Israel over all nations is clearly shown. The humiliation of the pagan kings, the salvation of Daniel from the lions' den, and the rescue of the three friends from the fiery furnace may have the appearance of wonder stories. But they are clearly intended as historical records of God's saving power beyond the boundaries of the now defunct promised land. The central theme of Daniel is in chapter 7:13–18, as the Son of Man receives dominion and power from God and shares it with the saints of the Most High. In the trauma of the Babylonian exile, God is showing that his saving purposes cannot be thwarted by pagan nations, however strong they are. Nor are they disabled by the fall of the promised land.

The second part of the book of Isaiah (Isa. 40 – 66) deals specifically with the return from the Babylonian exile and the future kingdom of God. Once again, we see that the people of God were not alone in their exile; the way back to their land is a way to be prepared for the Lord himself:

A voice cries:
'In the wilderness prepare the way of the LORD;
    make straight in the desert a highway for our God.

Every valley shall be lifted up,
> and every mountain and hill be made low;

the uneven ground shall become level,
> and the rough places a plain.

And the glory of the LORD shall be revealed,
> and all flesh shall see it together
>> for the mouth of the LORD has spoken.'

Isa. 40:3–5

God is with his people as he brings them back from their exile (Isa. 43:1–9,16–19). It is fitting that Mark should introduce the gospel and its herald, John the Baptist, with the quotes from Malachi 3:1 and Isaiah 40:3 (Mark 1:1–3; see also Luke 1:76 and John 1:23). John the Baptist proclaims the coming of the Lord to redeem his people from their exile and to bring them into his kingdom. But until the arrival of that moment announced by the prophets and John, the tribulations of the Jews under the Persians, the Greeks and then the Romans make it quite clear that, in Judea, they continue to be in exile.

Christians Yet Are Homeless Exiles Longing for Rest

So, we return to the exile of the Son of God. Jesus meets us in the world outside Eden that he might bring us with all his people back into the paradise of God. After Pentecost Jesus is absent from us in heaven, but remains present with us by his word and his Spirit. His promises to take his people to his home to be with him and the Father point to the eschatological hope that we expect to be fulfilled either when we die or when Jesus returns, whichever comes first.

Three themes are especially relevant. The first is the alienation Christians experience from a world that is at enmity with God. It will be marked by hatred and tribulation:

Then they will deliver you up to tribulation and put you to death, and you will be hated by all nations for my name's sake.

Matt. 24:9

For in those days there will be such tribulation as has not been from the beginning of the creation that God created until now, and never will be.

Mark 13:19

The reason why the world does not know us is that it did not know him.

1 John 3:1

For I consider the sufferings of this present time are not worth comparing with the glory that is to be revealed to us.

Rom. 8:18

Peter, an apostle of Jesus Christ, To those who are *elect exiles* of the dispersion in Pontus, Galatia, Cappadocia, Asia, and Bithynia, according to the foreknowledge of God the Father . . .

1 Pet. 1:1–2[11]

I, John, your brother and partner in the tribulation and the kingdom and the patient endurance that are in Jesus . . .

Rev. 1:9

---

[11] Italics mine.

Belonging to Jesus means that we have become enemies in the eyes of a world that refuses to submit to God. Thus, as Peter remarks, believers are exiles (1 Pet. 1:1; 2:11). Consequently, his reference to the fact that the resurrection of Jesus secures a new birth to a living hope is a significant encouragement (1 Pet. 1:3). This, of course, brings many tensions because we must go on living in this world. Fitting into our environment while at the same time remaining consistent to our heavenly home is not always easy. Some have tried to solve the matter by withdrawing from the world into the seclusion of monasteries or other places of permanent retreat. Mostly, Christians recognize that we are in the world to be salt and light; to proclaim the gospel to a needy humanity (Matt. 5:13–16).

A second theme that belongs with being an exile is slavery. Many of the older English versions of the Bible used the term 'serve' and 'servant' which, in many contexts, means 'slavery' and is so translated in other later versions. The stronger connotation of 'slavery' is appropriate in many places where servitude or bondage is clearly implied. So, in Hebrews 2:14–15, Christ has partaken of our predicament so that he might free us from slavery (ESV, KJV: bondage. See also Rom. 8:15,21; Gal. 4:9,24–26; 5:1). The analogy with the Old Testament is clear: exile to Egypt and to Babylon together provided a focus on the real meaning of being in exile from Eden. This is the slavery from which Christ came to set us free. If we follow the 'plot-line' of Hebrews, it starts with Jesus as superior to the angels, yet he is content to become one of those who are 'made lower than the angels' so that he might deliver us from the slavery to the devil and the fear of death (Heb. 1 – 2). This naturally leads on to the consideration of the early salvation history in Israel and the fact that Jesus is superior to its mediator, Moses. Israel failed to find its rest because of disobedience but, because of Christ's superior ministry as God's Son, there is now the promise of a Sabbath rest for his people (Heb. 3 – 4). Christ rescues us from all slavery to bring us to the true Sabbath rest.

A third and related theme is that of the inner tension we experience brought about by the fact that the old nature of sin, or the 'flesh', is at war with the Spirit. The word 'flesh' is used in some contexts simply to designate the human body or our humanness: 'And the Word became flesh and dwelt among us' (John 1:14). Paul describes his gospel as 'concerning his Son, who was descended from David according to the flesh' (Rom. 1:3). More relevant to our study is the use of 'flesh' to designate the inclinations of sinful humanity. It is opposed to what is spiritual, what is of God:

> For we know that the law is spiritual, but I am of the flesh, sold under sin.
>
> *Rom. 7:14*

> For I know that nothing good dwells in me, that is, in my flesh.
>
> *Rom. 7:18*

> For the mind that is set on the flesh is hostile to God, for it does not submit to God's law; indeed, it cannot. Those who are in the flesh cannot please God. You, however, are not in the flesh but in the Spirit, if in fact the Spirit of God dwells in you.
>
> *Rom. 8:7–9*

> For the desires of the flesh are against the Spirit, and the desires of the Spirit are against the flesh, for these are opposed to each other, to keep you from doing the things you want to do.
>
> *Gal. 5:17*

This tension affects every Christian and will not be resolved until we are in glory. It is part of the reality of being of the kingdom but not yet in it. It is the reason for the commands and encouragements in the New Testament to live godly lives. It is also the reason that a distinction is often made between our being holy in Christ and our needing to strive for holiness within ourselves.[12]

Both these factors, our alienation from the world and our internal struggles, impress upon us the fact that we are not yet at home nor at rest:

> For we know that if the tent that is our earthly home is destroyed, we have a building from God, a house not made with hands, eternal in the heavens. For in this tent we groan, longing to put on our heavenly dwelling . . .
>
> *2 Cor. 5:1–2*

> So we are always of good courage. We know that while we are at home in the body we are away from the Lord, for we walk by faith, not by sight. Yes, we are of good courage, and we would rather be away from the body and at home with the Lord.
>
> *2 Cor. 5:6–8*

We must conclude from all this that the exile of God's people is not over yet. That is why through the centuries Christians have

---

[12] Our positional sanctification (perfection) is attributed to us who are justified in Christ, whereby his merits are attributed to the believer. Our actual sanctification affects our empirical lives in which we must seek to put to death that which is earthly in us (Col. 3:5).

confessed with confidence: 'We look for the resurrection of the dead, and the life of the world to come.'[13] Our confidence is that Jesus has come into our exile to liberate us, and that God has shared the exile of his people from the moment our first parents were exiled from the Garden of Eden.

---

[13] Nicene Creed.

4

The City as Humankind's First Futile Attempt to Find Rest without God

The city may seem to be an unlikely theme when dealing with the Sabbath rest. It is a theme that emerges perhaps unexpectedly early in the narrative of the exile from Eden. The story of the biblical city has been a matter of interest for Christians since the apostolic age. The two cities of the book of Revelation will be familiar to most; the harlot city of Babylon is in stark contrast with the heavenly Jerusalem. There are three cities with theological significance in the New Testament: the old Jerusalem, significantly restored over the years since the Jews' return from the Babylonian exile; the new and heavenly Jerusalem as the ultimate destination of God's people; and the repository of all evil, the city of Babylon. The city is presented first in Genesis 4 as humankind's attempt to find rest without God. God's eventual answer to this is his holy city. You may have heard of Augustine's great work *The City of God* (*De Civitate Dei*). This is celebrated for being an early Christian philosophy of history. Augustine lived from 354 to 430. *The City of God* was written between 413 and 427. It included a defence of Christianity against the charge that its repudiation of the gods of Rome caused the decline of the Roman Empire.

More recently the subject of the city has been studied by biblical and systematic theologians.[1] I am not concerned here to deal with the sociological and spiritual challenges of urbanization. Rather, for this study, we need to consider the theological implications of the city as we find them in the Bible. We discover that certain cities of the ancient world figure in the revelation of God's purposes to bring in his kingdom.

The City in the New Testament

The massive urbanization of populations is a modern demographic phenomenon of planet Earth. Cities are ancient, but the immense megalopolis, with a population of millions, is a comparatively recent development. It is not only in newly industrialized countries that rural populations gravitate to the cities. The megalopolis is now a feature of modern society that echoes the gravitational pull of the black holes in space. Nothing can resist its force and everything seems to be swallowed up in it.

But cities have always featured in the organization of societies for various reasons. In the New Testament, cities are a fact of human existence in the world as it was then. But here the focus is more on the people of God, and especially on Jesus, who lived during the amalgamation of Middle Eastern and Greco-Roman

---

[1] For example: Jacques Ellul, *The Meaning of the City* (Grand Rapids, MI: Eerdmans, 1970); James Montgomery Boice, *Foundations of the Christian Faith* (Downers Grove, IL: InterVarsity Press, rev. edn, 1986), Part III A, 'A Tale of Two Cities'; B.T. Arnold, 'City, Citizenship', in *New Dictionary of Biblical Theology* (Leicester/ Downers Grove, IL: Inter-Varsity Press/InterVarsity Press, 2000), pp. 414–16.

cultures of the first century. While Jesus is referred to as a Nazarene (Matt. 2:23), and although he moves from town to town, he is not portrayed primarily as a city dweller. Rather, the gospels emphasize the crisis in his ministry when 'he set his face to go to Jerusalem' (Luke 9:51,53; see also Matt. 16:21; 20:18; Mark 10:33). But this great city for him is not the place of refuge or belonging, but where he must suffer and be put to death. It is no longer the holy City of God that we read of in the Old Testament. It is the place where, in an act of judgment, Jesus must cleanse the temple and, in so doing, put himself into conflict with the Jewish leaders (Matt. 21:12–13). And it is the city over which he will weep because it has missed its opportunity to find salvation (Matt. 23:37–39). He predicts the desolation that will come and the destruction of the city's great temple. Eventually, his enemies take him outside the city walls and put him to death. The tragedy of Jerusalem is that what was once the city of David should come to this; it becomes the place of the ultimate exile and alienation of the holy Son of God.

The city, or town, is also the place where Jesus warns that the gospel messengers will meet opposition:

And if anyone will not receive you or listen to your words, shake off the dust from your feet when you leave that house or town. Truly, I say to you, it will be more bearable on the day of judgement for the land of Sodom and Gomorrah than for that town.

Matt. 10:14–15

When they persecute you in one town, flee to the next, for truly, I say to you, you will not have gone through all the towns of Israel before the Son of Man comes.

Matt. 10:23

To state the obvious, cities and towns are where the people are. Cities become the concentration of human sinfulness. And there is an inherent perversity expressed in these towns when those whom Jesus designates as 'the lost sheep of Israel' (Matt. 10:6–7) assert their resistance to the message of restoration and salvation from the God of Israel. So, Jesus pronounces woes upon these cities:

> Then he began to denounce the cities where most of his mighty works had been done, because they did not repent. 'Woe to you, Chorazin! Woe to you, Bethsaida! For if the mighty works done in you had been done in Tyre and Sidon, they would have repented long ago in sackcloth and ashes. But I tell you, it will be more bearable on the day of judgement for Tyre and Sidon than for you. And you, Capernaum, will you be exalted to heaven? You will be brought down to Hades. For if the mighty works done in you had been done in Sodom, it would have remained until this day. But I tell you that it will be more tolerable on the day of judgment for the land of Sodom than for you.'
>
> *Matt. 11:20–24*

The significance of Sodom, Gomorrah, Tyre and Sidon would have been known to the biblically literate Jews whom Jesus addressed. He condemns Capernaum because it seeks to imitate the self-aggrandizement of Babel (Gen. 11:4). The city, then, is the place where Jesus confronts people with his works, but also is the centre of godlessness and resistance to the gospel.

Centuries before this, Israel's prophets had indicated that one day a renewed Jerusalem would emerge after the trauma of the Babylonian exile. However, the emphasis was more particularly on the new temple than on the city as such. How, then, does the New Testament deal with such prophetic expectations? Jesus weeps over Jerusalem and its lost opportunities. As he looks to the future, his only vision for Jerusalem is its destruction. Nowhere does he propose that this city will be restored and glorified. The so-called *little apocalypses* in the three synoptic gospels[2] do not support any kind of a literalist interpretation of Old Testament prophecies of a renewed Jerusalem here on earth. On the contrary, the focus is on the destruction of the temple and, by implication, the destruction of Jerusalem. The predictions in Matthew 24:1–31 are prefaced by Jesus weeping over Jerusalem. Mark 13:1–27 is parallel to Matthew's account, but Luke 21:5–24 extends his description of the devastation of the temple to the city. A literal fulfilment of prophecies concerning the future rebuilding of the old earthly Jerusalem or temple is nowhere to be found in the New Testament's eschatological vision.

If, as the Old Testament asserts, the city is the home of God's people, we must look elsewhere for another city. Hebrews shows us where to look by stressing that the patriarchs were looking ahead to a heavenly city. Observe how the city and the idea of a home country, or land of promise, are linked in the passage in Hebrews that deals with the faith of God's elect:

By faith Abraham obeyed when he was called to go out to a place that he was to receive as an inheritance. And he went out, not knowing where he was going. By faith he went to live in the land of promise, as in a foreign land, living in tents with Isaac and Jacob, heirs with him of the same promise. For he was looking forward to the city that has foundations, whose designer and builder is God.

Heb. 11:8–10

---

[2] These are the passages in which Jesus foretells the breaking into history of critical future events: Matt. 24; Mark 13; Luke 21.

Abraham is said to look forward to the city that Christians are also urged to seek (Heb. 13:13–14). Hebrews tells us that the land of promise is a foreign place for Abraham. The city of Abraham's faith is to be built by God himself. We are not told of its exact nature, but it is linked with the heavenly country. The fact that Abraham and his family did not experience the fulfilment of the promise is interpreted by Hebrews thus:

> These all died in faith, not having received the things promised, but having seen them and greeted them from afar, and having acknowledged that they were strangers and exiles on the earth. For people who speak thus make it clear that they are seeking a homeland. If they had been thinking of that land from which they had gone out, they would have had opportunity to return. But as it is, they desire a better country, that is, a heavenly one. Therefore God is not ashamed to be called their God, for he has prepared for them a city.
>
> *Heb. 11:13–16*

The principle is the same for homeland and city: the earthy expressions that were the subjects of the promise foreshadow the reality that is of heavenly origins. Did Abraham understand that the promises concerning the inheritance of Canaan were not the ultimate reality? Though the texts in Genesis do not suggest this, they turn out to be only the foreshadowing. But, because Abraham believed these promises, the writer of Hebrews is content to speak of him as having grasped the reality of the heavenly home. This is the usual New Testament perspective on Old Testament promise: those who grasped the original promise by faith are regarded as having grasped the future reality of its fulfilment.[3]

---

3   For example, see Gal. 3:7–9. In more general terms, the gospel is the message of the Old Testament; see Rom. 1:1–4; 3:21–22.

On this basis it is quite meaningful to say that the saints of the Old Testament were saved by faith in Jesus even though they had not heard his name.

For Paul, the cities of the empire are the places to which he must go with the gospel message of salvation. Where the cities are, the people are. Of course, in biblical times some cities were considerable population centres, but few, if any, approached the size we would associate with the city in modern times. No doubt places like Athens and Corinth, with their pagan cultures, presented a challenge to the evangelistic endeavours, and to the ongoing existence, of the newly established churches. But there is no obvious theology of the city itself in the epistles, not even in Paul's letter to the Romans. The cities of Paul's ministry are the cultural and demographic centres of ancient civilizations: they are the backdrop to the New Testament epistles, but no more than that. They would have affected the conditions that the new Christian communities had to cope with, but they did not feature in any way in the eschatology of Paul's epistles. Paul's missionary motive is not the city as such and its renewal, but rather his calling to take the gospel to the Gentiles.

But the city also raises questions about the fulfilment of prophecy, since Jerusalem and the temple figure so prominently in the eschatology of the prophets of Israel. One frequently made proposal is that all prophecy must be fulfilled in a completely literal way. I judge this to be an interpretative principle that sounds reasonable, even self-evident, but which proceeds on an unsound basis. Literalism can be a very subjective matter. As a principle of interpretation, it is rationalistic. To assert that 'God says what he means and means what he says' is a cliché without substance. A fully literalistic outcome would be impossible at the level of details.[4] We should draw our interpretative principles from the Bible itself. That means that we should allow the New Testament to dictate the way we interpret the Old Testament. The principle of interpretation then becomes, not literalistic, but Christological.[5]

The fulfilment of Old Testament prophecy is expressed in the letter to the Hebrews as a present reality for the people to whom this letter is written. It is generally held that Hebrews was written to Jewish Christians who were in danger of regressing to their old Judaism. The writer seeks to reassure them that they have truly reached their goal in Christ:

> But you have come to Mount Zion and to the city of the living God, the heavenly Jerusalem, and to innumerable angels in festal gathering, and to the assembly of the firstborn who are enrolled in heaven, and to God, the judge of all, and to the spirits of the righteous made perfect, and to Jesus, the mediator of a new covenant, and to the sprinkled blood that speaks a better word than the blood of Abel.

Heb. 12:22–24

Thus, while the book of Revelation looks forward to the consummation by taking up the contrast between the harlot city

---

[4] As clearly shown by Archibald Hughes, *A New Heaven and a New Earth* (London: Marshall, Morgan and Scott, 1958), pp. 155–61. See also Vern S. Poythress, *Understanding Dispensationalists* (Grand Rapids, MI: Zondervan, 1987), chs 8 and 9.

[5] Some dismiss this as 'replacement theology', but it is better understood as 'fulfilment theology'. Literalists also consider it a mortal blow to their opponents to write this off as 'spiritualizing'. In fact, it simply recognizes the spiritual dimensions of the antitype. In that sense, the New Testament does spiritualize Old Testament prophecy.

Babylon and the new Jerusalem, Hebrews speaks of believers as having already arrived in the heavenly Jerusalem.[6] This perspective is like Paul's in referring to believers as having reached the goal in Christ.[7] In Revelation the city emerges again as central to the deeds of God in bringing in his kingdom.

We may well ask why it is that Jesus focuses on the destruction of the great city of Jerusalem and of its temple. Why do the apostles apparently change the terminology of where God dwells with his people? The answer lies in the fact that the Old Testament imagery of land, city and temple are all fulfilled by Christ, and in him. Why, then, does John return to the imagery of the city in his last great vision of glory in Revelation 21 – 22? I suggest that the answer lies in the vision of the kingdom of God that is given clarity by the person and work of Jesus in whom all the Old Testament promises of God find their 'Yes' (2 Cor. 1:20). The apocalyptic imagery in Revelation graphically reconnects the gospel truths with their antecedents in the Old Testament promises. This reinterpretation by Jesus of those promises brings out with absolute clarity the divide that goes right back to the beginning of humankind's exile in the Old Testament. It is a divide between the godless and the godly, between unbelief and faith, between the elect and the non-elect. The city in the New Testament thus takes on a purely eschatological significance. Babylon's destruction and the coming of the heavenly Jerusalem are apocalyptic expressions of the final triumph of God's justice and the separation of evil from his kingdom for ever. To explain this further we need to return to the background to the New Testament's understanding of the city.

---

[6] The word 'city' features more than twenty-five times in Revelation.
[7] This perspective is found, for example, in Eph. 2:4–6; Col. 3:1–4.

It is commonly held that John's references to Babylon are veiled threats of divine retribution on Rome. This may be so, but I suggest that John's vision is wider than that. It must surely include all the cities that have become centres of godlessness, violence, immorality and every kind of evil. Athens, Corinth and even old Jerusalem qualify for this condemnation and the destruction threatened in Revelation 18. The fact that the Jews to whom John writes are under Roman domination, and thus continue to be exiles from God's holy city, makes Rome a prime target of this apocalyptically coded letter. God's ultimate answer to this violent age is the new and heavenly Jerusalem.

The Ambiguity of the City in the Old Testament

What, then, lies behind these New Testament perspectives on the city? Why is there a focus on the city of evil and the holy city of God? In our exile within this fallen and broken world, we experience and participate in the civilizations that we are part of by birth or by choice. Most of us retain a sense of belonging to the place in which we were born and grew up. While we adapt to developments and changes, we should be aware that, for God's people, the danger accompanying such adaptation was then, and is now, ever present. Our real home is a heavenly country and a heavenly city (Phil. 3:20), hence Paul's appeal to 'put to death therefore what is earthly in you' (Col. 3:5).

In the Old Testament, the city appears as a central feature of the social life of people outside Eden. When Cain murdered Abel, his punishment was to become a fugitive and a wanderer on the earth (Gen. 4:12,16). Human evil, then, brings about an exile within the exile; it compounds the plight of human beings outside Eden. Cain fled from the presence of the Lord to the land of Nod (Hebrew: *nod*, wandering). Wherever Nod was thought to be, it was for Cain initially a place of no home. It is also a deliberate attempt to get further away from God. Does this mean that Cain can have no home? In absolute terms, it does, for he is outside Eden. Is there any place more homeless than where he started: outside the garden? It turns out that there is. The fallen world is home where a fallen humanity lives, and people relate to other people and to the world. Cain forgoes this measure of belongingness by his murder of Abel. One of the features of home is relationships with people. Cain, the murderer, initially repudiates such relationships including that of being 'my brother's keeper'. Nevertheless, he is not content to be the perpetual wanderer, and he adapts to his new environment. He takes a wife and begets a son whose name he gives to the city that he builds (Gen. 4:17). This is a surprising development given Cain's initial lack of connections. For this city becomes the centre of a culture that includes animal husbandry, music and technology (Gen. 4:20–22). Cain thinks he has a home that he has constructed to overcome his alienation from home. But this home can never bring him back to Eden and to fellowship with God. His situation is one of double jeopardy. Adam was driven away from Eden yet finds some measure of a home outside it. Cain is driven further out to be a fugitive and settles in Nod, east of Eden. And now a city is built. But it is not a true place of rest. The city will come more and more to characterize the idea of home for human beings outside Eden, yet it will constantly fail to be an authentic home until God himself acquires a city; not a wanderer's refuge but the place where God puts his name – the city of God. Meanwhile, the human desire is to flee from God as from the enemy.

The biblical account turns to the line from Adam to Noah, through Seth (Gen. 4:25–26; 5:1–32). By contrast, the line of

Cain appears to blend into the general run of humanity that comes anew under God's judgment in Noah's flood. After the flood the remnant of humanity in Noah's line is divided again into the lines of Shem, Ham and Japheth. Noah's curse on Ham points us to a godless line that will be the focus of human evil in the world (Gen. 9:22–25). Once again evil builds cities (Gen. 10:6–14); Nimrod builds Babel and Nineveh, two cities that will come back to haunt the people of God and to challenge the city of God. The cities of the fallen world will be characterized by strife, warfare, human cruelty, and oppression and slavery.

The early story of God's people continues with Shem's genealogy that leads us to Abram. We discover that this is the lineage marked out by the grace of God (Gen. 11:10–32). But before that, the city reappears with Babel (Gen. 11:1–9): 'Then they said, "Come, let us build ourselves a city and a tower with its top in the heavens, and let us make a name for ourselves, lest we be dispersed over the face of the whole earth"' (Gen. 11:4). This story emphasizes the desire to be independent of God. The human fear is that of being dispersed over the face of the earth. This desire for society without God is a corruption of the way God made humankind in his image; the image of the purest social being who is the divine and eternal Trinity. Ever since the expulsion from Eden, people have expressed their radical revolt against God by wanting to 'go it alone'; to 'milk' the image of God for the benefits of society, but without acknowledging God. Thus, outside Eden the human attitude is that we can maintain our independence of God and be free of his interference. Control over our own destiny without God's meddling is the constant desire of a rebellious humanity. The city is our way of expressing this independence. It is our way of trying to secure rest and certainty without God.

It represents and supports the aspirations of autonomous human beings. Great cities are the pride of a godless race. The Lord's response to Babel is to disperse the city builders and confuse their language 'so that they may not understand one another's speech' (Gen. 11:7). There is a theological pun in this event. *Shem* is the Hebrew word for 'name'. The descendants of Shem were chosen by God and would bear his name. But here is a godless rabble of people who want to make a 'shem', a name, for themselves without God. The result is Babel: the confusion of languages.

The call of Abram comes with the promises of a nation and a land in which to dwell. There is no sign of a city at this point. There is rather an echo of Eden in which the idea of a city would have been discordant. Canaan is not Eden, but nor is it Nod. Abram's descendants will dwell there and experience the blessing of God (Gen. 12:1–3; 13:14–17). The power of the godless city will have to be challenged by God's man, as the narrative now shows us. When Abram's nephew, Lot, settles among the cities of the valley, he puts himself in danger of the evil that is there (Gen. 13:12–13). Lot, now dwelling in Sodom, is captured by the forces of a coalition of kings (probably tribal sheiks) but is rescued by Abram (Gen. 14:11–16). Lot's rescue from the evils of Sodom will have to be repeated later, and we may wonder at his suicidal propensity to get involved with these centres of wickedness (Gen. 19:1–38).

But this first account of Lot's misfortunes is notable for the contrast of the cities and their kings. After Abram's successful expedition, the kings of Sodom and of Salem come to meet him (Gen. 14:17–18). The evil of Sodom needs no further comment, and Abram is firm in wanting no favours from its king. By contrast, Melchizedek, king of Salem, blesses Abram who, in turn, gives tithes to the king. We are left in no doubt about the significance of Melchizedek. Salem is generally accepted as ancient Jerusalem, which will one day be nominated as the city of God. Melchizedek is identified as both king of the city and a priest of God Most High (Hebrew: *'el 'elyon*). Abram identifies God Most High as Yahweh, and there is no doubt that we are intended to see Melchizedek as a priest to Abram's God (Gen. 14:22).

Two cities now occupy our line of sight; two cities that represent the best and the worst of the situation in the fallen world outside Eden. The mysterious figure of Melchizedek will emerge again in relation to the theme of the priesthood (Ps. 110:4; Heb. 6:20 – 7:25). But here he appears as one link between the promises to Abram and the city of Jerusalem. This link will lie dormant until the ascendancy of King David nearly a millennium later. David will be God's man to bring this city into the centre of saving history where it will become the city of God. God will promise David that he will have rest in the land, of which the city of God is made the centre (2 Sam. 7:10–11). Meanwhile the evils of Sodom will characterize the harlot city of Babel-Babylon as it emerges to be the destroyer of all good things.

We are left in no doubt about Sodom's place in the order of things, and it is surely significant that the narrative weaves the account of Sodom's destruction into the account of the covenant with Abram. Abram refuses anything from the king of Sodom lest he should say, 'I have made Abram rich' (Gen. 14:22–24). And then the word of the Lord comes to the yet childless Abram, reinforcing the promises made earlier of a nation of his descendants (Gen. 15:1–6). Again, God speaks to 99-year-old Abram, promising that he will become 'father of a multitude of nations' (Gen. 17:1–8). His name is changed to Abraham to signify this.[8] The birth of Isaac is promised to fulfil God's covenant assurances (Gen. 17:19). It is then that we are told of the three visitors to Abraham (angels?) who once again reinforce the covenant promise (Gen. 18:9–19). The visitors then announce their intention to go to Sodom, and it is evident that judgment is in the air. Although Abraham intercedes for Sodom, Lot's city will be destroyed. Lot is saved with his two daughters, but his wife is overtaken by the destruction (Gen. 19:23–29). The city of evil stands in stark contrast to the rural setting of Abraham the tent-dweller whose descendants will inhabit the land of promise.

Although we may think of Abraham's family as itinerant rural dwellers, it would be a mistake to judge all cities as inherently anti-God and to see the pastoral life as a kind of return to Eden. It is much more complex than that. Cities will figure in the life of God's people throughout the whole of redemptive history. It is the ambiguity of the city that is the problem. Cities will be part of the social organization of human beings and will function for good or ill. In Egypt, the slavery and oppression of the Hebrews is expressed by putting them to work building cities (Exod. 1:8–14). Yet, it had been grain stored in such cities that enabled Joseph to save his brothers from starvation (Gen. 41:46 – 42:4). In retrospect, the descent of Jacob's sons into Egypt is a covenantal necessity. Before they can enter the promised land, Israel must experience what it is to be redeemed by the mighty arm of God. They must be delivered from the cities of Egypt's gods, from slavery to an alien king, and from oppression in a land not their own. Slavery in Egypt is a focused microcosm of human experience of exile from Eden.

---

8   Abram means 'exalted father'; Abraham means 'father of a multitude'.

The exodus presents the people of Israel with the promise of the land that God is giving them. But they are going into a land with cities, and these cities are the places where strange and foreign gods are worshipped, and evil is practised in their name. It is this that condemns these cities. The Israelites are warned of the idolatry that characterizes the cities that they will capture:

> But in the cities of these peoples that the LORD your God is giving you for an inheritance, you shall save alive nothing that breathes, but you shall devote them to complete destruction, the Hittites and the Amorites, the Canaanites and the Perizzites, the Hivites and the Jebusites, as the LORD your God has commanded, that they may not teach you to do according to all their abominable practices that they have done for their gods, and so you sin against the LORD your God.
>
> *Deut. 20:16–18*

It is here that we see the rationale for the destruction of the dispossessed nations that for so many presents a moral problem.[9] The city is, from one point of view, nothing more than the bricks and mortar that people have constructed to enable themselves to survive as a social unit. It becomes a snare when it is allowed to continue as the place where human rebellion against God and the practice of evil is institutionalized.

---

[9] Of this kind of 'problem', John Bright comments: 'I find it most interesting and not a little odd that although the Old Testament on occasion offends our Christian feelings, it did not apparently offend Christ's "Christian feelings"! Could it really be that we are ethically and religiously more sensitive than he? Or is it perhaps that we do not view the Old Testament – and its God – as he did?' *The Authority of the Old Testament* (London: SCM Press, 1967), pp. 77f.

The Old Testament narrative does not reflect our modern notions of multiculturalism. The idea of competing religions existing side by side in tolerant acceptance of one another has no place in the early formation of Israel. There is good reason for this. At this stage in the history of redemption the absolute opposition of idolatry to the prophetically revealed truth must be emphasized. Cities are part of the human social scene, but a city can be used for God or against him:

> And when the LORD your God brings you into the land that he swore to your fathers, to Abraham, to Isaac, and to Jacob, to give you – with great and good cities that you did not build, and houses full of all good things that you did not fill, and cisterns that you did not dig, and vineyards and olive trees that you did not plant – and when you eat and are full, then take care lest you forget the LORD, who brought you out of the land of Egypt, out of the house of slavery.
>
> *Deut. 6:10–12*

So, the danger was always there; the structures of civilization could cause the people of Israel to forget the Lord. They did not enter the promised land as if it were pristine and undeveloped. The problem was not only that they could forget that all the good things came from the Lord, but that they could be contaminated by the idolatry and evil practices of the inhabitants. Time would show that such contamination was more easily accepted than one might have anticipated at the time of the entry into Canaan.

The already existing snare of idolatry was the reason for the principle of the 'devoted thing' (Hebrew: *ḥerem*) that was imposed. The Israelites could not survive in the land if a comprehensive scorched earth policy were to be enforced. So, instead, certain places were chosen by God for destruction, to remind Israel of the need to avoid the contamination that could happen so easily when they took over the cities of the idolatrous Canaanites. The principle is clearly asserted that cities are there and the Israelites will live in them. But:

> If you hear in one of your cities, which the LORD your God is giving you to dwell there, that certain worthless fellows have gone out among you and have drawn away the inhabitants of their city, saying, 'Let us go and serve other gods', which you have not known, then you shall enquire and make search and ask diligently. And behold, if it be true and certain that such an abomination has been done among you, you shall surely put the inhabitants of that city to the sword, devoting it to destruction, all who are in it and its cattle, with the edge of the sword. You shall gather all its spoil into the midst of its open square and burn the city and all its spoil with fire, as a whole burnt offering to the LORD your God. It shall be a heap for ever. It shall not be built again. None of the devoted things shall stick to your hand, that the LORD may turn from the fierceness of his anger and show you mercy and have compassion on you and multiply you, as he swore to your fathers . . .
>
> *Deut. 13:12–17*

This provision may seem to us unnecessarily severe, but we should understand that so much was at stake here: the whole future of God's gospel-salvation. The principle of the devoted thing was like a fumigation against the plague that is needed to save the rest of the population. Several things begin to converge here. The city, with its potential for idolatry, lies in stark contrast to the place that 'the LORD your God will choose out of all your tribes to put his name and make his habitation there' (Deut. 12:5). We will learn that one specially chosen city will be the place where God puts his name and makes his dwelling in the temple. Meanwhile, when Joshua leads the people over the Jordan into the promised land the city of Jericho is designated as a devoted thing. Achan defies the ban and is condemned to be part of the devoted thing himself. Israel pays for its sin in being defeated in the battle for Ai (Josh. 7:1–26).

This survey of the city in the lives of the people of God illustrates the basic fact that there is a division of humankind between those who are the objects of God's grace and those who continue in culpable rebellion against God. The division of the two lines began with Cain and Abel. In Genesis, the two lines are expressed in terms of the genealogies and in human attitudes to God.[10] The cities initially are described as expressions of human wickedness, but the situation changes when Israel takes possession of the Jebusite city of Jerusalem and it becomes the city of God. Cities can be the focus of either godliness or ungodliness. They become representations of the condition of humankind before God.

The City of God and the House of God

After their escape from the cities of Egypt – which is an escape from the dominion of foreign gods and powers – the Israelites become wanderers in the wilderness (Num. 14:1–35). Their faithlessness results in a whole generation condemned to exist in a desert limbo, Israel's Nod, until permitted to enter the promised land and to possess its cities. The allocation of tribal

---

[10] See the discussion of the two lines of humankind in my book *Gospel and Kingdom*, now in *The Goldsworthy Trilogy* (Milton Keynes: Paternoster, 2000), pp. 64–6.

regions, described in the book of Joshua, does not result in the total dispossession of the respective Canaanite inhabitants (Judg. 1:27–36). While Judah captures and burns Jerusalem (Judg. 1:8), the men of Benjamin fail to drive out its Jebusite inhabitants, who continue to possess the city until David takes it (Judg. 1:21; 2 Sam. 5:6–10).

The city and the sanctuary are naturally linked. We hear nothing of the wilderness tabernacle after the commissioning of Joshua to succeed Moses as leader of Israel (Deut. 31:14–15,23). The first book of Samuel informs us of the sanctuary that is now at Shiloh. Samuel's ministry begins here but, as in the book of Joshua, the emphasis is on the ark of the covenant as the tangible guarantee of God's presence with Israel. The history of the ark in the period dealt with in 1 Samuel is not our immediate concern. Its disastrous capture by the Philistines and subsequent return can be followed in 1 Samuel 4:1 – 7:2. The significance of the ark is amplified when David captures Jerusalem and then brings it to the city (2 Sam. 6:1–23). The narrative of 2 Samuel 7 is crucial to the whole theology of the king, the city and the temple.

First, we note that David is unhappy that the ark dwells in a tent (2 Sam. 7:1–3). We do not know what happened to the temple at Shiloh. The wilderness tabernacle was portable because the people were travellers not yet settled in the land promised to them. Joshua 18:1 indicates that the tabernacle was set up in Shiloh as a more enduring situation, yet still temporary. But the land was intended to be a permanent dwelling place; cities were inevitable and one of them was destined to be the city of God. David is right to recognize the incongruity of the primary witness of God's presence remaining in a temporary dwelling.

Second, David's concern to provide a fitting house for the ark leads to the verbal ambiguity of the word 'house' being exploited in the narrative. Arguably the theological high-point of the narrative in 2 Samuel, the question of a house for God now involves us in the other kind of house: a dynasty of God's anointed kings. God's house and David's house will continue in tandem until the heir in David's dynasty is revealed as also the dwelling of God: Immanuel (2 Sam. 7:4–17). Jesus, as Son of David and as the new temple, combines the two meanings of 'house' in himself.

There is little doubt that a city came to be associated with the god or gods of its inhabitants. The passage quoted above (Deut. 13:12–17) puts idolatry squarely within the cities of the Canaanites that the Israelites were to possess. It is hardly surprising that once the city becomes the centre of human social development and intellectual endeavour, it also becomes the centre of religion. The creation of gods and their temples, in other words *religion*, is the final expression of independence from God the Creator:

Claiming to be wise, they became fools, and exchanged the glory of the immortal God for images resembling mortal man and birds and animals and creeping things. Therefore God gave them up in the lusts of their hearts to impurity, to the dishonouring of their bodies among themselves, because they exchanged the truth about God for a lie and worshipped and served the creature rather than the Creator, who is blessed for ever! Amen.

Rom. 1:22–25

The relationship of the temple to the city is more than the result of social forces. The temple or sanctuary of a god or gods represents the presence of the deity among the people. There is an association of power and the gods. Idolatry (religion) is the corrupt imitation of God and his power.

The beginning and the ending of the biblical narrative both contain an interesting similarity alongside an important difference. In Eden there is no city or temple, while in the heavenly Jerusalem there is no temple but a city that embraces the river of life and the tree of life (both images of Eden). Between the beginning and the end of the biblical story one city has emerged as the principal metaphor of God's presence among his people. If we follow the biblical history of the city, perhaps we can propose at least one reason why this is.

The history of the city, which I have summarized above, begins without explanation. Adam and Eve in the garden cannot constitute a city although, as a family unit, they form the embryonic precursor to a city. When Cain murders Abel he becomes a fugitive from the presence of the Lord. He marries, and builds a city (Gen. 4:16–17). From that point onwards, the city represents the concentration of human wickedness. Noah curses his son Ham for his sin, and the outcome is the building of Babel and Nineveh, among other cities. Both these cities will be prominent in the afflictions of God's people. Neither Shem nor Japheth are recorded as city builders (Gen. 10:1–5,21–32). The city and the tower of Babel (Gen. 11:1–9) are fundamental expressions of human independence of God. The resulting confusion of languages addresses this urban manifestation of evil. Urbanization expresses increasing secularization, and the confusion of languages restrains its development. These narratives provide the background to the phenomenon of the ancient city-state associated with the religious expressions of godlessness.

By contrast with the godless cities, Jerusalem figures prominently in the eschatology of the prophets of Israel.[11] The theme

---

[11] Often Jerusalem is designated by its spiritual-theological title, Zion. Some relevant prophecies are Isa. 2:2–5; 4:2–6; 28:16; 30:18–19; 33:5–6,20–22; 35:10; 40:1–11; 46:13; 51:3,11; 52:1–2, 7–8; 60:14; 62:1,11–12.

of Isaiah has been summarized by Barry Webb as 'Zion in Transformation'.[12] The prophecy begins with a description of the doomed Jerusalem (chapter 1) and then indicates the glorious Zion that will one day emerge (chapter 2):

It shall come to pass in the latter days
  that the mountain of the house of the LORD
shall be established as the highest of the mountains,
  and shall be lifted up above the hills;
and all the nations shall flow to it,
  and many peoples shall come, and say:
'Come, let us go up to the mountain of the LORD,
  to the house of the God of Jacob,
that he may teach us his ways
  and that we may walk in his paths.'
For out of Zion shall go the law,
  and the word of the LORD from Jerusalem.

Isa. 2:2–3

The restoration of Jerusalem and the temple is an important prophetic theme. The question then arises as to the fulfilment of these prophetic passages, a question that we must allow the New Testament to answer for us.

How does the city come to be integral to the purposes of God and emerge finally as the principal metaphor of the kingdom of God in Revelation 21? Our survey of the city shows it to be the centre of human evil. Jacques Ellul makes the striking

---

[12] Barry Webb, 'Zion in Transformation: A Literary Approach to Isaiah', in *The Bible in Three Dimensions* (ed. D. Clines et al.; Sheffield: JSOT Press, 1990); Barry Webb, *The Message of Isaiah*, The Bible Speaks Today (Leicester: Inter-Varsity Press, 1996).

proposition that God has taken over the city in the redemption effected by Jesus Christ:

> But then this contradiction arises: the Judeo-Christian concep-
> tion which shows that all of man's works, summed up in the city,
> are included in the glorious new state of re-creation, also shows
> that it is not by man's work that this event will come about . . .
> There are two directions to be followed, both of which are basic to
> the history of the city. One originates in Cain, the other in Eden,
> and they converge finally in the new Jerusalem. Each expresses
> one form of the saving and kingly act of God in Jesus Christ.[13]

The history of God's people certainly supports this assessment. Exile to the cities of Egypt is addressed by the redemption of the exodus. Set before the Israelites is the promise of
the land and its cities with all the potential for influencing
them for evil (Deut. 6:10–12). The book of Joshua relates
the process of conquest of these cities in Canaan. At his fare-
well, Joshua describes the conquest as the fulfilment of the
promises of God: 'And now I am about to go the way of all
the earth, and you know in your hearts and souls, all of you,
that not one word has failed of all the good things that the
LORD your God promised concerning you. All have come to
pass for you; not one of them has failed' (Josh. 23:14). His
last words are a stern warning against breaking the covenant;
an act of faithlessness that will bring this judgment: '[Y]ou
shall perish quickly from off the good land that he has given
to you' (Josh. 23:16).

The climax of the process of possession comes with David's
victories and his dispossession of the Jebusites from their city

---

[13] Ellul, *The Meaning of the City*, p. 163.

of Jerusalem. It becomes the city of David and, when the ark of the covenant is brought into it, the city of God.[14] Thus the city, the very heart of humankind's declaration of independence from God, becomes the focal point of the revelation of God's kingdom. God enters the very centre of our rebellion against him, and redeems it to be his own dwelling among us. Jerusalem marks the redemption of the city. The capstone is put in place with the building of Solomon's temple. Thus all the elements have converged in this last great earthly foreshadowing of a heavenly kingdom.

The tragedy of Jerusalem is that, having become the city of God, it forsakes the privilege and honour it has received and becomes corrupt and apostate. The most poignant expression of this is found in the book of Lamentations. But even here, in the horror of God's judgment, there is the note of hope:

> The punishment of your iniquity,
> > O daughter of Zion, is accomplished;
> he will keep you in exile no longer . . .

Lam. 4:22

The city of Jerusalem, destroyed because of idolatry and apostasy, will be restored. It will remain for the New Testament to show us how that restoration will occur.

In the light of the significance of Zion, the city of God, it is not surprising that it is linked with the people of God entering their rest. When we bear in mind that Zion, or Jerusalem, is the focal point of the promised land, finding rest in the land

---

[14] The city of God is referred to in Pss 46:4; 48:1,8; 87:3; Isa. 60:14 (the 'City of the LORD').

is but a foretaste of the rest that is found in the city. By entering the promised land, God's people will have rest (Deut. 3:20). God promises, through Moses, that in the place where he will put his name, they will have rest (Deut. 12:10). We later discover this place is the city of Jerusalem, the centre of the promised land:

> But when you go over the Jordan and live in the land that the LORD your God is giving you to inherit, and when he gives you rest from all your enemies around, so that you live in safety, then to the place that the LORD your God will choose, to make his name dwell there, there you shall bring all that I command you: your burnt offerings and your sacrifices . . .
>
> *Deut. 12:10–11; see also Deut. 25:19*

At first, the land is indeed the place of rest (Josh. 1:13–15; 21:43–45; 22:4; 23:1). But, when David captures Jerusalem, everything about the land that signifies salvation is focused on the city; the place where God causes his name to dwell (2 Sam. 7:1,9–14). This process also involves David's name (*shem*) being made great (v. 9) in a way that shows his succession to the status of Abraham (Gen. 12:1–3). After David, Solomon recognizes that his rest means he can build the temple (1 Kgs 5:2–5; 1 Chr. 22:8–10,17–19; 23:25; 2 Chr. 20:28–30). Ideally, then, the city of God represented the salvation-rest for the people of God. We know the ideal never became the reality, and what imperfect rest they achieved in that place was squandered through disobedience and idolatry.

The significance of Jerusalem, the city of God, is often extolled in the Psalms. Several psalms have been described as 'Zion hymns', and contain a rich theology of the city chosen by God as his dwelling.[15] This is not the place for a detailed examination of such psalms, but we should be aware of the way Zion became the focus of celebration and the praise of God. Psalm 46 was the inspiration for Luther's famous hymn, 'A Mighty Fortress Is Our God'.[16] The psalm celebrates the security of those who dwell in this unshakeable fortress. Psalm 48 speaks of Zion as the place that exemplifies the eternal joy and safety enjoyed by its citizens. Psalm 87 shows Zion as the place where even the Gentiles may find salvation and shelter.

Notwithstanding all this positive reflection on the real meaning of Zion or Jerusalem, idolatry and covenant-breaking lead to the devastation of God's people. We met Nineveh in Genesis 10:11–12 as a city of the Hamites. We hear little of this Assyrian city until the commissioning of the prophet Jonah to go and preach repentance to this evil place. Given that Jonah is identified as living during the first part of the eighth century BC, the outcome presents us with a problem. His mission is successful in that the Ninevites repent and judgment is averted. This is a puzzle when we realize that the Assyrians were to destroy the northern kingdom of Israel around 722, not long after their so-called repentance. Clearly, the Assyrians did not become Yahweh worshippers alongside the faithful Israelites and people of Judah. Perhaps Jonah's mission was God's way of showing idolatrous Israel that, if need be, he can raise up children to Abraham even among the Ninevites. John the Baptist

---

[15] More than thirty psalms refer to Zion, but those that can be regarded as hymns to Zion include Pss 46; 48; 76; 84; 87; 122. See Leopold Sabourin, *The Psalms: Their Origin and Meaning* (New York: Alba House, 1974).

[16] Another English version of Luther's hymn is a more literal translation of Ps. 46:1: 'God is our refuge and strength'.

uses a similar argument to the Jews who plead descent from Abraham: 'God is able from these stones to raise up children for Abraham' (Matt. 3:9). Nineveh's role in the destruction of Israel is not the last we hear of this city. Its destruction is forecast in the prophecies of Nahum and Zephaniah. Jesus refers to the sign of Jonah as denoting his resurrection, and the fact that Ninevites will judge the unfaithful of Israel (Matt. 12:38–41).

The New Jerusalem and Its Temple

Both the biblical history and prophetic eschatology show us that Jerusalem was only an earthly and representative expression of the presence of God. For all its importance, it nevertheless fails and is destroyed. After the Babylonians plunder the city in 586 BC, only the prophetic promise remains; a promise that will find fulfilment in the very presence of God in the true temple (John 2:19–22). Then, in John's apocalyptic style, we have the reintroduction of the images of the Old Testament in the book of Revelation. The New Testament thus provides clear links with the prophetic significance of the historical Israel, and at the same time incorporates the transformation of these images to the person of Jesus. In other words, as the land, the city and the temple in Israel are fulfilled in Christ, the value of the earthly imagery is transformed in Revelation to the heavenly origins of the Christian's final home: the new Jerusalem descending to the new earth.

The final question to ponder is this: how do the city and the temple figure in the life of the Christian? Since the significance of God's city is found in the temple, the temple is likely to be more prominent in the New Testament. The city is redeemed by Christ, who is also revealed as the new temple. The presence of God among his people is the presence of Christ, first in the flesh, and then by his word and Spirit. The same word and Spirit create the reality of the body of Christ, the church. This is not the place to explore the doctrine of the church but, in the New Testament, the Old Testament idea of the people of God in the city of God with its temple is transformed into the people of God in Christ. After the ascension of Jesus, the literal earthly city of Jerusalem and its temple have no more place in the New Testament language of the kingdom of God. The epistles are silent about any future restoration of these linked with the return of Christ.

The temple imagery is applied thus: Christ is the new temple, and those united to Christ by faith share in the temple's reality. God dwells amid his faithful servants, who thus become temples of the Holy Spirit. On an individual basis, the Christian's body is a member of Christ and should be honoured as such (1 Cor. 6:14–15). The Spirit dwells within us and we are thus reminded that we do not have ownership of that which God has bought with a price (1 Cor. 6:19–20). The temple is also a corporate reality that defines Christian existence. Paul's concern to clarify the relationship of Jew and Gentile under the gospel is expressed in Ephesians 2:11–22. Gentiles, who were strangers to Israel's covenants of promise, have been brought near in Christ. The result is that believers from both sides are now joined together and grow into a holy temple. They are 'being built together into a dwelling place for God by the Spirit'. The predications belonging to the city and the temple in the Old Testament are given their true significance in Christ (Eph. 2:21–22; 1 Pet. 2:4–8).

The book of Revelation reintroduces the heavenly Jerusalem as the new Eden where God dwells with his people. In the first Eden there was no temple because God was there with his people and there was no barrier between them caused by their sin. There was no need in Eden for a mediatorial ministry to provide forgiveness and fellowship. Similarly, in the new Jerusalem there is no temple, 'for its temple is the Lord God the Almighty and the Lamb' (Rev. 21:22). Christians are at home in this use of Old Testament imagery to describe our life in Christ, as John Newton does in his famous hymn:

> Glorious things of thee are spoken,
>   Zion, city of our God![17]
> He whose word cannot be broken
>   formed thee for His own abode.
> On the Rock of Ages founded,
>   what can shake thy sure repose?
> With salvation's walls surrounded,
>   thou mayst smile at all thy foes.[18]

Newton goes on in the second verse to describe the grace of God as the sustaining river of living water and, in the third verse, declares us to be citizens of Zion:

> Saviour, since of Zion's city
>   I, through grace, a member am,
> Let the world deride or pity,
>   I will glory in Thy name:
> Fading is the worldling's pleasure,
>   All his boasted pomp and show,
> Solid joys and lasting treasure
>   None but Zion's children know.

---

[17] This line is from Ps. 87:3.

[18] John Newton (1725–1807).

As Ellul suggests,[19] God's redeeming work in Christ has given us a strong city (Isa. 26:1–4). Cain's city of refuge from the judgment of God was a futile gesture (Gen. 4:17), but the grace of God leads us through the earthly Jerusalem to the heavenly city of God. What we are shown in the New Testament is the fulfilling in Christ of the central Old Testament images of city and temple. Israel is redeemed from slavery and exile in Egypt and given the promised land. God's chosen messianic king, David, transforms the godless Jebusite city of Jerusalem into the city of God. God's messianic son, Solomon, is gifted to build the dwelling place for God, the temple. The three concentric circles – land, city and temple – express the presence of God dwelling with his people. All are fulfilled in Christ.

---

[19] See note 13 above.

5

The Sabbath Rest: Its Definition and the Promise of God-given Rest

In the application of the Ten Commandments, there is probably more disagreement among Christians about the significance of the Sabbath law than about any of the other nine. We can agree that the requirement for Israel's observance of the Sabbath day is contained in the Mosaic covenant at Sinai (Exod. 20:8–11). But its application to us as Christians is another matter. The stated rationale in Exodus is that God created everything in six days, and rested on the seventh day from his work of creation, as it is recorded in the Genesis account:

> Thus the heavens and the earth were finished, and all the host of them. And on the seventh day God finished his work that he had done, and he rested on the seventh day from all his work that he had done. So God blessed the seventh day and made it holy, because on it God rested from all his work that he had done in creation.
>
> *Gen. 2:1–3*

For centuries this passage has influenced the way many Christians have thought about a day of rest. It is frequently assumed that Sunday, the day of resurrection, should be regarded as the Christian Sabbath. If we are to understand what our attitude should be to one day's rest in seven, our first concern is to examine how the Sabbath is related to the ministry of Jesus.

Jesus and the Jewish Sabbath

As one who was raised in the Anglican tradition, I soon became familiar with the so-called 'comfortable words' that follow the confession and absolution[1] in the Holy Communion service of the Book of Common Prayer (1662): 'Hear what comfortable words our Saviour Christ saith unto all that truly turn to him. Come unto me all that travail and are heavy laden, and I will refresh you.'[2] In this context it seems that the Anglican Reformers took these words to be an assurance of sins forgiven. That always had appeared to me to be the natural interpretation of what Jesus was saying about rest or refreshment. By roundabout means, this interpretation may have real strength; but the biblical context points us in a different, if related, direction.

In this passage, Jesus offers rest to those who labour and are heavy laden and who come to him (Matt. 11:28). But isn't working what is expected of us? 'Six days you shall labour, and do all your work' (Exod. 20:9). The requirement to work is followed by the provision of the Sabbath rest (Exod. 20:10). So, to whom is Jesus speaking and what is he offering? The use

---

[1] The absolution consists of a declaration that God forgives the sins of those who truly repent and believe the gospel.

[2] KJV, ESV and others: 'I will give you rest.' The BCP quotation from Matt. 11:28 is followed by the second of the comfortable words which is John 3:16. Later revisions of the Prayer Book have changed to the KJV rendition.

of these words of Jesus in the Anglican liturgy removes it from its wider context in Matthew's gospel. Here it is a good idea if we ignore the numbering of chapters, which were added later and certainly are not original to Matthew's gospel. This saying (Matt. 11:28–30) makes better sense if it is read as part of the two Sabbath pericopes that follow. Matthew goes on to relate words that Jesus had about the Sabbath and Pharisaic legalism (Matt. 12:1–8). In this context it seems that Jesus addresses those who are burdened by such Pharisaic legalism and who need to experience the rest which results from becoming his disciple. But being his disciple was no pushover! This rest is better understood as deliverance from the futile and burdensome concerns that had clouded the Jewish understanding of the real significance of God's commands.

Jesus clearly regarded himself as a law-abiding Jew. But he differed in at least three ways from the average Jewish aspirational law-keeper. First, he claimed to perfectly fulfil the law; a unique claim that goes way beyond merely endeavouring to keep the law (Matt. 5:17). Second, he was the only Jew who ever did keep the law, fully, always, and perfectly (Heb. 4:14–15; 5:7–10; 7:15–28). Yet his contemporaries often regarded his behaviour as the very opposite to perfect obedience; he was accused of being a blasphemer and a law-breaker. Third, he took it upon himself to interpret, in a definitive way, what it meant to keep God's law as it was meant to be kept. In this he often found himself at odds with the general community expectations of good and acceptable Jewishness. The conflicts that were generated between Jesus and the religious leaders of his day were frequently a result of the growing divide between his claims to be doing the Father's will, and the increasing trend towards a legalistic interpretation of Judaism that was eventually to lead to developed Rabbinic Judaism.

From the time of Moses onwards, the keeping of the Sabbath was regarded as the centre of the observance of the law. As we shall see later in examining the Sabbath in the Old Testament, its observance was a critical issue for the people of God. In the gospels, the Sabbath appears to be a significant cause of conflict between Jesus and the religious leaders. Wilfrid Stott has proposed that Jesus clearly broke with the emerging rabbinic traditions concerning the law and the Sabbath, but in doing so he never hinted at the annulment of the observance of the day.[3] The references to Jesus and the Sabbath in the gospels focus on the differing interpretations placed on keeping this law. Stott enumerates six confrontations relating to Jesus and his actions, mostly healings, on the Sabbath that illustrate this:

1. The disciples plucking grain on the Sabbath (Matt. 12:1–8; Mark 2:23–28; Luke 6:1–5);
2. The healing of the man with the withered hand (Matt. 12: 9–14; Mark 3:1–6; Luke 6:6–11);
3. The healing of the woman with a disabling spirit (Luke 13: 10–17);
4. The healing of the man with dropsy (Luke 14:1–6);
5. The healing of the man invalided for thirty-eight years (John 5:1–17);
6. The healing of the man born blind (John 9:1–41).

Apart from these controversial incidents, there are other references to Jesus attending the synagogue on the Sabbath day, which Luke says was 'his custom' (Luke 4:16). It is hardly

---

[3] Wilfrid Stott, 'Sabbath', in *The New International Dictionary of New Testament Theology* (ed. Colin Brown; Exeter: Paternoster, 1978), 3:405–11.

surprising that he would attend the synagogue at Nazareth if the assembly was to be an opportunity for his teaching and healing. It is significant that it is on the Sabbath that Jesus declares that he fulfils the prophecy of the coming salvation (Luke 4:16–21, quoting Isa. 61:1–2). This passage in Luke goes on to relate the healing of the man possessed by an unclean demon, which takes place on a Sabbath in Capernaum (Luke 4:31–37). But, if it was his custom to attend synagogue, it suggests he regularly attended the meetings because that is what Jews did as part of the Sabbath observance.

The issue that emerges is not that Sabbath observance was wrong, but that many Jews had come to invest it with a legalistic straitjacket that hindered its proper use. The question then concerns the original God-given purpose and meaning of the Sabbath day, and how the corruption of this had developed over the centuries so that Jesus is portrayed as having a quite different understanding of the true meaning of the Sabbath from that held by the Jewish teachers of his day.

The incident of the hungry disciples plucking grain on the Sabbath is reported in the three synoptic gospels.[4] The Pharisees challenge this use of the Sabbath as unlawful. The response of Jesus is to justify the disciples' actions on the grounds of David's eating of the bread of the Presence in the house of God (1 Sam. 21:1–6). All three accounts record how Jesus claims that 'the Son of Man is Lord of the Sabbath' (Matt. 12:8; Mark 2:28; Luke 6:5). This would have been a very provocative statement. While there has been much discussion about the use of the term 'the Son of Man' by Jesus, it seems to make little sense

---

[4] The synoptic gospels are Matthew, Mark and Luke; so called because of their similarity of approach which contrasts with John's gospel.

in the contexts of the gospels if he is only signifying 'human being', the literal meaning in both Hebrew and Aramaic. It is safe to assume that Jesus is identifying with the heavenly Son of Man in Daniel 7 who receives power and authority from God. If this is so, then Jesus is claiming supreme authority to say what is involved in keeping the Sabbath and what is not.

Only Matthew includes the significant statement of Jesus that the priests are guiltless when they profane the Sabbath at the temple, and that 'something greater than the temple is here' (Matt. 12:5–6). The implication is that Jesus is the one greater than the temple. This claim is like his enigmatic reference to his fulfilling of the temple scriptures in John 2:18–22. Only Mark includes the statement, 'The Sabbath was made for man, not man for the Sabbath' (Mark 2:27). This may refer to the fact that humans were created before the Sabbath law was given at Sinai. It is more likely that Jesus refers to the goodness of God in his provision for his people. The law was given to God's people, who had been redeemed through the miracles of the exodus. It was never a programme to achieve redemption but rather was given to structure the already redeemed life. Since the Sabbath was made to serve human beings, to benefit another human being on the Sabbath is clearly lawful. Matthew's account, including the reference to the one who is 'greater than the temple', points us in the direction of the coming of the eschatological age so clearly promised in the Old Testament.

The problem of the healings that Jesus performs on the Sabbath also brings us to the claim that the Day of the Lord is here. If, as seems likely, Jesus went out of his way to heal on the Sabbath, we have a good indication that the Sabbath, like the temple, has eschatological significance; it points to the coming fullness of God's kingdom. While many healing miracles that Jesus did are not specified as being on the Sabbath, when he did heal on that day it caused much controversy and brought him into conflict with the Jewish authorities. Clearly the Sabbath is not to be taken as a day of legalistic restriction, but a day that signified the healing and liberation of the Day of the Lord. When John the Baptist was in prison he sent word to Jesus: 'Are you the one who is to come, or shall we look for another?' Jesus responded: 'Go and tell John what you hear and see: the blind receive their sight and the lame walk, lepers are cleansed and the deaf hear, and the dead are raised up, and the poor have good news preached to them' (Matt. 11:4–5). While Jesus healed on other days, it seems that his work of healing on the Sabbath highlights what accompanies the coming of the Lord.

The Sabbath Law for Israel

The way Jesus dealt with the question of the Sabbath is based on the giving of the Mosaic law in the Old Testament. The creation story tells of God finishing his work and resting on the seventh day, but there is no specific mention of a Sabbath for God's people until Exodus 16:22–26. This event, involving the gathering of the wilderness manna, occurs after the exodus from Egypt and before the Sinai covenant and the giving of the Ten Commandments. On the sixth day the Israelites were to gather twice as much manna and to desist on the seventh, the Sabbath. We are not told when such a Sabbath rule was given, and there is no mention of a Sabbath observance before this event.

At Sinai the people gather at the mountain and Moses mediates the instruction that God gives him. This Sinai law[5]

---

[5] Hebrew: *torah*. The word comes from a root that indicates instruction. Here it is binding because it is instruction given by Yahweh to direct the lives of his redeemed people.

appears to have been anticipated in that Yahweh has already instructed his people in such matters. The word we translate as 'law' first occurs in Genesis when the covenant blessings are relayed to Isaac: 'Because Abraham obeyed my voice and kept my charge, my commandments, my statutes, and my laws' (Gen. 26:5). We do not have any record in Genesis of a Sabbath law or any other specific instruction being given to the patriarch but, clearly, it must have happened. There is nothing to indicate in what measure this instruction was the same as the Sinai covenant. However, in the same manner as Sinai, this instruction is for the benefit of God's covenanted people.

When the Ten Commandments are given along with the Book of the Covenant (Exod. 20:1 – 24:8), Israel has already experienced the event of redemption, the exodus from slavery in Egypt. This occurrence provides the pattern of God's grace in salvation from that time onwards all the way into the New Testament (Exod. 20:1–2). The Sabbath commandment is the longest of the ten:

> Remember the Sabbath day, to keep it holy. Six days you shall labour, and do all your work, but the seventh day is a Sabbath to the LORD your God. On it you shall not do any work, you, or your son, or your daughter, your male servant, or your female servant, or your livestock, or the sojourner who is within your gates. For in six days the LORD made heaven and earth, the sea, and all that is in them, and rested on the seventh day. Therefore the LORD blessed the Sabbath day and made it holy.
>
> *Exod. 20:8–11*

It is simplistic to take the reference to God resting on the seventh day after the creation as reason to assert that the Sabbath commandment is a 'creation ordinance'. The implication of this assessment is that God intended this law to be universally and permanently in force. No such law occurs in the creation text. Andrew Shead rightly points out that the commandment changes 'seventh' in Genesis 2:3 to 'Sabbath' in Exodus 20:11, and he warns us not to take this as equating the two days. He concludes the following: 'First, this commandment is not a mandate for Sabbath observance by all humanity, for the lesson of creation is applied narrowly to the Israelite Sabbath. Secondly, the basic reason given for Sabbath observance is the imitation of God. God's example of work which finds its completion in rest should be the model for Israel . . . There is more to life than work.'[6] That there is more to life than work is expressed in the words of Moses concerning the manna: 'man does not live by bread alone, but man lives by every word that comes from the mouth of the LORD' (Deut. 8:3, words that Jesus uses against Satan's temptation in Matt. 4:3–4).

The Sabbath is commanded with great solemnity by God as he speaks to Israel through Moses:

> You are to speak to the people of Israel and say, 'Above all you shall keep my Sabbaths, for this is a sign between me and you throughout your generations, that you may know that I, the LORD, sanctify you.'
>
> *Exod. 31:13*

> Therefore the people of Israel shall keep the Sabbath, observing the Sabbath throughout their generations, as a covenant for ever. It is a sign for ever between me and the people of Israel that in six

---

[6] 'Sabbath', in *New Dictionary of Biblical Theology* (ed. T.D. Alexander and Brian Rosner; Leicester/Downers Grove: Inter-Varsity Press/InterVarsity Press, 2000), p. 746.

days the LORD made heaven and earth, and on the seventh day he rested and was refreshed.

Exod. 31:16–17

There is no doubt that God intends Israel to take the Sabbath law extremely seriously as it is stressed in several places that the penalty for breaking it is death. As Calvin remarks, 'The Lord enjoined obedience to almost no other commandment as severely as to this [Num. 15:32–36; cf. Exod. 31:13ff.; 35:2].'[7] Nevertheless, I believe it is a mistake to read the simple statement of fact – God rested – and turn that into an ordinance of command. The Sabbath law is not a creation ordinance but a Sinai ordinance based on God's covenant with Israel.

When the next generation of Israelites is about to enter the promised land, Moses gives the 'second law' (Deuteronomy) which includes the Ten Commandments (Deut. 5:6–21). These are almost word for word the same as the Sinai version in Exodus 20 except in the Sabbath commandment. This time it is not the creation-rest that is used to give a rationale for the commandment, but the redemption from slavery in Egypt. This prompts us to ask what, if anything, links the seventh day of creation and the release from slavery since both are given as motives for Sabbath observance. Once again we see that the Sabbath is not a universal creation ordinance but something that is based on the covenant faithfulness of God to Israel. Thus, Scott Hafemann is right to reject Sabbatarianism: 'God's "rest" was the rest of satisfaction and a stamp of his approval on his work. As such, God "hallowed" the Sabbath, or set it apart, which is the same as

---

[7] John Calvin, *Institutes of the Christian Religion, vol. 1* (ed. John T. McNeill; trans. Ford Lewis Battles; Philadelphia: Westminster, 1960), II, 8, 29, p. 395.

saying he made it "holy" (Gen. 2:3; Exod. 20:11). The Sabbath was God's unique declaration of the good news that his provision for his people was perfect (Gen. 1:29–30).[8] He also takes account of the dynamics of redemptive history when he comments:

> I do not believe that the command given to Israel to keep a literal Sabbath must be kept by Christians, though of course a regular pattern of corporate worship is essential. Keeping the Sabbath under the old covenant was a symbolic reminder of the fundamental truths of creation and covenant, which are fulfilled under the new covenant in a life of faith-producing obedience seven days of [*sic*] week (Heb. 3:16 – 4:13). In Christ, every day is the Sabbath! With transformed hearts, we now keep the Sabbath by trusting in God to meet our needs in every circumstance, manifesting this faith by a life of growing contentment expressed in righteousness (1 Tim. 6:6–16).[9]

Hafemann rightly places the Sabbath commandment in the context of the covenant promises to Israel. Calvin has similar qualifications on the Sabbath: 'If one fears superstition, there was more danger in the Jewish holy days than in the Lord's days that Christians now keep. For, because it was expedient to overthrow superstition, the day sacred to the Jews was set aside; because it was necessary to maintain decorum, order, and peace in the church, another was appointed for that purpose.'[10]

---

[8] Scott J. Hafemann, *The God of Promise and the Life of Faith* (Wheaton, IL: Crossway, 2001), p. 45.

[9] Hafemann, *God of Promise*, p. 224, n. 4 to p. 44.

[10] Calvin, *Institutes* (ed. McNeill), II, 8, 33, p. 399. The editorial footnote points out that Calvin did not see the Lord's Day as a simple continuation of the Sabbath, 'but a distinctly Christian institution adopted on the abrogation of the former one, as a means of church order and spiritual health'.

To set aside observance of one day and replace it with another does not mean, despite any overlap of significance, that the replacement is simply a new form of the old.

Once we have established the covenant context of Sabbath, its relationship to the general notion of 'rest' in the promised land follows. There are two Hebrew roots that are predominantly used for 'rest'. That they are closely related in meaning is shown by the fact that references to the Sabbath day itself consistently use *šbt* but references to God resting or the people resting frequently use *nwḥ*, the two even occurring side by side. In Exodus 20:8–11, Israel is told to remember the Sabbath (Hebrew: *šbt*) because God rested (Hebrew: *nwḥ*) on the seventh day. The outcome of the exodus from Egypt was intended to be the possession of the Promised Land, thus fulfilling the covenant promise made to Abraham. When the Israelites come to the land and eventually take possession of it and establish the glorious kingdom of David and Solomon, they are said to have been given rest (Hebrew: *mᵉnuḥah*,[11] rest [1 Kgs 8:56; 1 Chr. 22:9; Ps. 132: 8–14]). Meanwhile, the Sabbath commandment in Deuteronomy 5:12–15 indicates that a subsidiary purpose is to ensure that servants may also share that Sabbath rest (Deut. 5:14). The principle is extended to the land in the provision of the sabbatical year (Lev. 25:1–7). Both provisions can be taken as showing that God provides for the needs of his people in the promised land.

God clearly intended Israel to find rest in the land that he was giving to them:

> For you have not as yet come to the rest and to the inheritance that the LORD your God is giving you. But when you go over

---

[11] *mᵉnuḥah* is the noun formed from the verb *nwḥ*.

the Jordan and live in the land that the LORD your God is giving you to inherit, and when he gives you rest from all your enemies around, so that you live in safety, then to the place that the LORD your God will choose, to make his name dwell there, there you shall bring all that I command you . . .

Deut. 12:9–11

But this rest was dependent on Israel's obedience to the covenant. The covenant curses in Deuteronomy 28 threaten the scattering of the faithless, and their consequent restlessness among the nations:

And the LORD will scatter you among all peoples, from one end of the earth to the other, and there you shall serve other gods of wood and stone, which neither you nor your fathers have known. And among these nations you shall find no respite, and there shall be no resting-place for the sole of your foot, but the LORD will give you there a trembling heart and failing eyes and a languishing soul.

Deut. 28:64–65

Solomon acknowledges this link between promised land and rest in his great prayer of consecration of the temple: 'Blessed be the LORD who has given rest to his people Israel, according to all that he promised. Not one word has failed of all his good promise, which he spoke by Moses his servant. The LORD our God be with us, as he was with our fathers' (1 Kgs 8:56–57).

Conversely there is the terrible judgment pronounced in Psalm 95:11, which is referred to in Hebrews 3:7–19, that the rebellious 'shall not enter my rest'. There is also a convergence of related themes in Psalm 132:13–14. Here God's Sabbath rest refers to his dwelling in Zion:

> For the LORD has chosen Zion;
>> he has desired it for his dwelling place;
> 'This is my resting-place for ever;
>> here I will dwell, for I have desired it.'

At the heart of the promised land is the city of Zion and the temple. This is where Israel is to find rest and where God also rests. We cannot escape the echoes of God's rest on the seventh day and Israel's rest in the land of its inheritance. Here is the real significance of the Sabbath day's rest.

But even the glories of Solomon's temple in Zion are only symbolic of God's transcendence; God's people are not yet in the rest prepared for them. Solomon understands this:

> But will God indeed dwell on the earth? Behold, heaven and the highest heaven cannot contain you; how much less this house that I have built! Yet have regard to the prayer of your servant and to his plea, O LORD my God, listening to the cry and to the prayer that your servant prays before you this day, that your eyes may be open night and day towards this house, the place of which you have said, 'My name shall be there', that you may listen to the prayer that your servant offers towards this place.
>
> *1 Kgs 8:27–29*

God dwells in heaven, but it is enough that God has made his name to dwell in the Jerusalem temple; for the time being this is God's resting place.

To summarize: the Sabbath observance was a covenant obligation of Israel that paralleled the completion of God's creation in which God shows that all is done to provide for the needs of his people within that creation. It also receives motivation from the 'new creation' of Israel in the exodus. Eden is the prototype of the kingdom of God. Outside Eden, the promised land is the typological expression of the kingdom which finds its fulfilment in Jesus. To keep the Sabbath is to rest in him.

The Sabbath Rest for the People of God

We have seen how Jesus demonstrated that the growing legalism of Pharisaic Judaism had obscured the real significance of the Sabbath. It had come to symbolize restrictions on the freedom of the people and to stand in the way of the promise of God's kingdom. But it could be kept without such corruptions, as the words and actions of Jesus amply showed. The dynamics of the history of redemption include transitions from the time of anticipation of the coming of the kingdom to the reality as it is revealed in Jesus. We must thus account for the changes occurring at the advent of Jesus of Nazareth and at his ascension. The transition from Old Testament expectation to New Testament fulfilment was not instantaneously appreciated by the disciples of Jesus. For us, this is both a literary and historical matter as we move from the Old Testament scriptures to the New. It also presents us, above all, with a theological development of crucial significance. Sometimes Christ's people were slow to understand the changes until they were forced to by circumstances. And sometimes contemporary Christian comment fails to grasp this dynamic. The disciples continued at the temple and, it would appear, in seventh-day Sabbath observance until it was clear that it was time for a break.

The radical break came with the proclamation of the gospel after the ascension of Jesus and his giving of the Holy Spirit. One aspect of the transition was the growing appreciation of the covenant promises concerning the blessing to the Gentiles and their inclusion in the kingdom of God. These covenant promises concerning the Gentiles had apparently become muted in Judaism, a situation that carried over into the primitive Jewish Christian church. Peter's vision forces him to re-evaluate his attitude to the Gentiles and the giving of the Spirit to them (Acts 10:9–48). Subsequently, the Jerusalem council shows the first stages in the reassessment of the place of the Gentile believers in the church (Acts 15:1–35). All these events anticipate the problem of Judaizers in the churches. These were Jewish adherents to the churches who maintained that, since Christianity is Jewish and the fulfilment of Judaism, to become a Christian a Gentile must first become a Jew. In various ways Paul addresses this problem in several of his letters. The question of the relationship of the Gentiles to the Jewish law meant that the whole subject of the law had to be reconsidered for both Jewish and Gentile Christians. In the Old Testament, any Gentiles finding salvation did so through becoming attached to Israel and its institutions, including the temple and its services. But now the true temple is revealed as Jesus, and the man-made temple in Jerusalem not only becomes superfluous, it becomes a potential digression from the gospel.

In considering the Christian attitude to the Sabbath we must recognize that, though it was regarded as paramount in Jewish law-keeping, it was but one part of the entire law of Moses. References to the Sabbath in Paul's epistles are few: one direct mention in Colossians 2:16, and a general reference to the observance of days, months and seasons in Galatians 4:10.

In both cases Paul has only negative comments about a legalistic compulsion to observance:

> Therefore let no one pass judgement on you in questions of food and drink, or with regard to a festival or a new moon or a Sabbath. These are a shadow of the things to come, but the substance belongs to Christ.
>
> *Col. 2:16–17*

> But now that you have come to know God, or rather to be known by God, how can you turn back again to the weak and worthless elementary principles of the world, whose slaves you want to be once more? You observe days, and months and seasons and years! I am afraid I may have laboured over you in vain.
>
> *Gal. 4:9–11*

The context of both passages is Paul's understanding that Christ's coming means that the law of Moses no longer functions as the principal instrument of guidance of God's people. The shadow must give way to the reality as it is in Christ: 'So then, the law was our guardian until Christ came, in order that we might be justified by faith. But now that faith has come, we are no longer under a guardian, for in Christ Jesus you are all sons of God, through faith' (Gal. 3:24–26).

This is not the place to attempt a full treatment of Paul's understanding of the law and what it means that we are 'not under law but under grace' (Rom. 6:14). However, it is worth noting that Paul's treatment of justification by faith, apart from works of the law, leads him to say that this upholds the law (Rom. 3:28–31). This is because the righteousness of God is 'for all who believe' (Rom. 3:21–22); our justification is a gift merited by Christ alone (Rom. 3:23–26).

Our inability to keep the law was met by the perfection of Christ's obedience. Thus, faith in his doing and dying upholds the law of God (Rom. 3:31). We keep the Sabbath perfectly by faith in Jesus.

Another matter that embraced the whole question of Gentiles being required to keep the law was circumcision (Acts 15:1–5; Rom. 2:25–29; 4:9–15; Gal. 2:3–12; 5:1–6). Circumcision and Sabbath together show us that the law was not rigidly subdivided into ceremonial and moral sections as Protestants have tended to maintain in our time. The Thirty-nine Articles (Article VII), the Westminster Confession (Chapter XIX) and the Belgic Confession (Article XXV) are all examples of rather ambiguous expressions of the place of the law in the Christian life. They agree that the Old Testament law contained two types of commandments: ceremonial and moral. The moral laws are said to remain in place while the ceremonial laws are fulfilled in Christ and thus abrogated. It must be maintained that all are fulfilled in Christ. Do the moral laws remain because they are moral and not ceremonial? Under the grace of the gospel certain moral implications are essentially the same as those in the law of Moses. This is because they reflect the character of the one God. This does not mean we are still under the law of Sinai.

Nevertheless, the law was the law, and you either submitted to it or you didn't. It hardly needs saying that not being under the law does not imply lawlessness; we have the law of Christ (Gal. 6:2). Guidance, motivation for good deeds and enabling for the godly life all come from the gospel of grace applied by the Spirit (Gal. 5:16–26). We look now to Christ on Calvary, not to Moses on Sinai. This does not mean that we can simply dispense with the Old Testament; if for no other reason, we need it to understand what it is that Christ fulfils.

Not only do the New Testament epistles give no encouragement to Sabbatarianism, they say almost nothing about physical rest and recreation. The gospels also have only a few allusions to rest of a physical kind. For example, after a busy time of itinerant preaching the apostles report back to Jesus: 'The apostles returned to Jesus and told him all that they had done and taught. And he said to them, "Come away by yourselves to a desolate place and rest a while." For many were coming and going, and they had no leisure even to eat' (Mark 6:30–31). But we read then how that rest was disturbed by assembling crowds, and the work resumed. When Jesus came to the dead Lazarus, he commented that 'Lazarus has fallen asleep.' The disciples 'thought that he meant taking rest in sleep' (John 11:11–13). This is very different from the prescription of one Sabbath day off in seven. In the garden of Gethsemane, Jesus leaves the disciples to watch and pray while he goes alone to pray. Three times he returns to find them sleeping and rebukes them: 'So, could you not watch with me one hour?' and 'Sleep and take your rest later on. See, the hour is at hand, and the Son of Man is betrayed into the hands of sinners' (Matt. 26:40–45).

Let us recognize, then, that we cannot turn whatever we deem appropriate for Sunday into a Sabbath on the questionable grounds that Sabbath-keeping is said to be a creation ordinance. It is far more consistent with Paul's theology of the law to say that it was instituted 'until faith should come' and that Christians 'are not under law but under grace'. For Christians, the meaning of the Sabbath remains, but it is transformed by the gospel. The evidence indicates that it took some time for the implications of the gospel to bring about the changes that we now take for granted. Meanwhile we deem it appropriate to use the Lord's Day for meeting together (Heb. 10:24–25). That does not make Sunday a Christian Sabbath. After all, the Sabbath commandment says nothing about what an Israelite was obliged to do on that day other than to keep it holy; it only prohibits work. I suspect that mostly we tend to interpret the holiness of Sunday in accord with personal preference or the recently formed traditions of our local Christian subculture.

As the apostle to the Gentiles, Paul never urged either circumcision or Sabbath-keeping on his converts or the churches. There is no way that the Sabbath could have escaped Paul's reappraisal of the law in the light of the gospel. The unbelieving Jews who had persecuted and killed Stephen had failed to grasp that the essence of Stephen's message was that they should move on from the old structures and embrace the fulfilment of law and the temple in Jesus Christ (Acts 6:8 – 7:53). It seems that the Jewish Christians in the Jerusalem church were also finding it difficult to see how the death and resurrection of Jesus affected their attitude to the law and to the Gentiles. Peter's vision (Acts 10:9–16) and the Jerusalem council (Acts 15:1–35) demonstrate the problems the first Jewish Christians had in making the transition.

Does the Sabbath simply die at the hands of Paul? It is true that he mentions it by name only once to clarify the implications of the gospel for freedom from bondage to the law. But he has other ways of pointing to the implications of the gospel for the Old Testament themes we have examined. Israel's observance of the Sabbath was motivated by the fact that God rested after creating his people, establishing their relationships, and providing all that was needed for meaningful life before God. It was also motivated by redemption from slavery for freedom in the new Eden-like rest of the Promised Land. The Sabbath law was the regularized way to express dependence on the goodness of God's provision for his chosen people. The Sabbath thus signified the rest that God gave and always promised to give; a rest that meant life in the presence of God in the good land he gives. Sabbath, or rest, was to express the stability of kingdom existence: God's people in God's land under God's rule and provision.

It is this theme that is followed up in the epistle to the Hebrews. The superiority of the ministry of Jesus to that of Moses is one prominent motif in that letter. In this context (Heb. 3:1–19) the warning is given against unbelief; a hardness of heart that will disqualify one from entering the rest. The assurance is given: 'There remains a Sabbath rest for the people of God, for whoever has entered God's rest has also rested from his works as God did from his' (Heb. 4:9–10). The thrust of Psalm 95, to which Hebrews refers, is that Israel forfeited its rest because of hardness of heart:

> Today, if you will hear his voice,
> > do not harden your hearts, as at Meribah,
> > as on the day at Massah in the wilderness,
> when your fathers put me to the test
> > and put me to the proof, though they had seen my work.
> For forty years I loathed that generation
> > and said, 'They are a people who go astray in their heart,
> > and they have not known my ways.'
> Therefore I swore in my wrath,
> > 'They shall not enter my rest.'
>
> > > > *Ps. 95:7–11, quoted in Heb. 3:7–11*

The promised land spoke of Israel's rest: it foreshadowed a return to an Eden-like rest. The psalmist urges those of his generation to learn from this and not follow their forebears in unbelief and hardness of heart. Hebrews then applies the same warning to Christians:

> For we have come to share in Christ, if indeed we hold our original confidence firm to the end. As it is said,
>
> > 'Today, if you hear his voice,
> > Do not harden your hearts as in the rebellion.'
> >
> > *Heb. 3:14–15*

> Therefore, while the promise of entering his rest still stands, let us fear lest any of you should seem to have failed to reach it.
>
> *Heb. 4:1*

> Let us therefore strive to enter that rest, so that no one may fall by the same sort of disobedience. For the word of God is living and active, sharper than any two-edged sword, piercing to the division of soul and of spirit, of joints and of marrow, and discerning the thoughts and intentions of the heart.
>
> *Heb. 4:11–12*

The dynamics of this Sabbath rest are clearly rehearsed in Hebrews 4:4–11. Its foundation is in God's resting on the seventh day of the creation (v. 4). Psalm 95 recalls the wrath of God over the disobedience of the Israelites after the exodus when they refused to enter God's rest in the land (v. 5). But David's psalm does not leave it as an historical memory of the days of Moses; it contemporizes it to 'today' in the ongoing situation of God's people (vv. 6–7). So much was said about 'rest' in relationship to the entry into Canaan under Joshua, but the fact that God spoke of 'another day later on' (v. 8) means that the rest that God promises is yet to be attained.

The eschatological rest indicates that, at best, the rest in the land was but a shadow of the rest that comes from entering the true rest through Christ (vv. 9–16). The promise of the eschatological rest is placed alongside the threat of not entering it because of the faithlessness of the disobedient (v. 11). And, lest any should think that God will overlook disobedience, we are reminded of the fact that we cannot escape the power of God's word that exposes all our nakedness (vv. 12–13).

In Revelation, John views the matter from the perspective of those who have already entered their rest. He uses vivid apocalyptic metaphors, based on the Old Testament, to describe the blessedness of what we call heaven. In Revelation 7 he sees the 144,000 from the twelve tribes of Israel who are sealed for God. Here is symbolized the perfect number of elect Israel. This is followed by the vision of the great multitude that no one could number, gathered from every nation, tribe and language group. These are all standing before the throne of God and the Lamb. In Revelation 14, John again describes the 144,000 before the Lamb on Mount Zion. This vision is followed by that of three angels with messages of judgment and salvation. Then the word of assurance: 'Here is a call for the endurance of the saints, those who keep the commandments of God and their faith in Jesus. And I heard a voice from heaven saying, "Write this: Blessed are the dead who die in the Lord from now on." "Blessed indeed," says the Spirit, "that they may rest from their labours, for their deeds follow them!"' (Rev. 14:12–13).

For Christians, then, the Sabbath law is not a direction concerning what to do, and what not to do, on Sunday. Rather it is the essence of the eschatological hope of eternal rest. On the seventh day of creation God rested in the sense that he had achieved his goal of a perfect universe with humankind at its centre. His rest signified that the creation was 'very good'.

Everything had been done to ensure that the creation was cared for and nurtured, and that humanity had all that it needed for a full and meaningful existence before God. There was a divine equilibrium in all creation: everything was as it should be. For us, the Sabbath rest speaks of a similar perfection that is to come. It speaks of a new creation that is the fulfilment of Eden and the promised land, and is the realm of eternal life.

6

The Authentic Christian Life of Rest While Still Moving towards Our Rest

As I began this study, I commented that relationships provide the grounds for attributing meaning to our existence. The account of creation in Genesis 1 – 2 defines us, and thus gives us our true meaning in terms of foundational relationships with God, with others of our species and with the world around us. The sobering account in Genesis 3 of the human rebellion against God's lordship tells of humanity's rejection of these relationships. Yet, by the mercy of God, the exile from Eden that follows is not the end of our story. Exile from Eden also becomes a journey for those called and redeemed by God, a journey that leads back to the promised land and the true Sabbath rest.

Our Choice of Agendas: Biblical or Secular

The well-known hymn 'Guide Me, O Thou Great Jehovah' turns to some of the imagery we have been considering:

When I tread the verge of Jordan,
Bid my anxious fears subside;

Death of death, and hell's destruction,
Land me safe on Canaan's side;
>   Songs of praises
>   I will ever give to Thee.[1]

The idea that the life of faith is a journey leading to the very presence of God and of his Christ is frequently expressed in Scripture and in Christian literature and hymnody. The biblical imagery in the hymn 'Guide Me, O Thou Great Jehovah' is based on the narrative of the Israelites' redemption from Egypt and eventual entry into the promised land. The Christian is described as a 'pilgrim through this barren land'. In verse 2 the writer prays, 'Let the fire and cloudy pillar lead me all my journey through'.[2] The imagery of crossing Jordan quoted above describes the end of the Christian's pilgrimage to heaven; the true promised land that Canaan could only dimly foreshadow. It turns up in various Christian expressions of the believer being in sight of or about to enter the promised land, however that is conceived of in Christian terms. Crossing the Jordan has become a recognizable metaphor for going through death to enter the presence of God in heaven. Rivers and mountains can also express the trials of the exiles' journey to the promised land. One version of the well-known spiritual 'One More River to Cross' concludes thus:

And I've got one more river
I've got one more river
I've got one more mountain

---

[1]   Verse 3 of the hymn 'Guide Me, O Thou Great Jehovah' by William Williams, 1745.

[2]   Exod. 13:21–22; 40:36–38; Num. 9:15–17.

Before I take my rest.
Heavy burdens down here
They all make just a-one more river
Trials is a-one more river
Disappointments is a-one more mountain
Before I take my rest.

The analogy with Israel's wilderness journey towards the promised land is implied in this song.

As we come to consider the results of this study on the Sabbath rest, we need to reflect on its value for us now as we seek to live the Christian life authentically, that is biblically, in a world that has so much going for it and yet does not know us because it does not know God (1 John 3:1). The New Testament constantly reminds us of the tension between the 'now' and the 'not yet'; between being in this world while belonging to the kingdom of God. It is a tension between flesh and spirit, between this world and the world to come. It is a tension between our justification and our experiential sanctification and spiritual maturity. How we are doing in the life of faith should always be a concern, even though our justification is based on the achievements of Jesus on our behalf. These tensions, and how we deal with them, affect a great deal. If we are unclear about the nature of our journey to the goal we call heaven, we will most likely be unable to find assurance that we are on the right path.

Assembling the Pieces

In this study, I have selected some of the possible themes that could contribute to our understanding of what it means to journey towards our goal of eternal life with God. We looked first at the cause that made a journey necessary; why we are 'not there yet', but rather are travelling towards the desired end. The sin of our first parents resulted in their expulsion from Eden under the sentence of death. The theme of the exile is pervasive in Scripture but not triumphant. Grace has intervened and God has led his elect on the way that leads to Christ and eternal life.

The next step in this study was to examine the idea of the city and its place in the human attempt to find home while in exile from God's kingdom. We saw how the grace of God again intervenes and his city, Jerusalem, becomes a redemptive image of the dwelling of God among his people. Connected with the city is the foreshadowing of rest in the Promised Land and the presence of God with his people which is expressed by the temple.

Finally, I sought to expound the notion of God's rest and the way this motivates the Sabbath principles in both the Old and the New Testament. We saw how the keeping of the Sabbath was a specific requirement for the Israelites under the law of Moses. But the coming of Jesus brought important modifications to the requirements of the law. We noted the way that the old Sabbath law foreshadowed the eternal rest of the people of God that still lies ahead of us.

Following these chosen themes in order, we can see that there are various ways we can link them to express a basic unity in the biblical accounts. Thus: expulsion from Eden raises the matter of human rebellion against the creative grace of God and against the supreme authority of the Creator. Outside Eden, humanity is homeless but mercifully preserved by God, who then implements a gracious plan of salvation. Until the consummation of God's redemptive plan there remains a real sense that we are all homeless. Even when we have been incorporated into the body of God's elect and made his children by adoption and grace, we are still far from home in this world. Of course, in Christ we have already arrived, but in ourselves we are still on the way. The remarkable thing about the gospel is that it tells us of the amazing grace of God demonstrated in the coming of Jesus to share our exile and homelessness in order to bring us home.

In chapter 3 we focused on the idea of exile and homelessness. The kingdom of God in prototype was seen in the created perfection of Eden and the life of Adam and Eve with God; a relationship that established *all* relationships that give meaning to human existence. The rebellion against this order led to the disorder of exile, and to the completely undeserved grace of God in his progressively revealed plan of redemption. The building blocks that we looked at in biblical order were:

- Eden as home with God
- Rebellion resulting in judgment
- Exile from Eden
- The covenant of grace and redemption in the exodus
- The Promised Land: foreshadowing the place of rest
- Rebellion and idolatry in the land, resulting in exile in Babylon
- Israel's return from one exile to what is still an exile
- God in exile with us in Jesus
- Redemption and the promise of home for eternity
- The 'meanwhile' Christian life in exile.

From this we see that the people of God through the ages experienced in various ways the foreshadowing of the ultimate expressions of judgment, exile, homelessness, redemption and rest in the kingdom.

In chapter 4 we examined the idea of the city. Cities have been a fact of human society from ancient times. It may come as a surprise to some to find that there is a definite biblical theology of the city that informs us of the purpose and spiritual value of the cities in redemptive history, and their connection with the metaphors of eternal life. Again, we looked at the pieces in biblical order:

- Expulsion, and the first city of Cain
- Increasing evil and the tower of Babel
- Sodom and Gomorrah: centres of human evil
- Israel's exodus from the cities of Egypt
- God gives the cities of the Canaanites to Israel
- Babylon as the focal point of evil
- The city of David becomes the city of God
- Jerusalem and the temple
- Jesus, the new temple
- Jerusalem forsakes the new temple
- The destruction of Jerusalem and the temple
- The city of God: new Jerusalem.

Outside Eden, the city becomes the centre of human evil. But it is also the place where human society develops and expresses its own creativeness. It is not obliterated in the plan of God. Rather, the city is redeemed through the capture of a pagan city by God's anointed king, David, and becomes the place where God puts his name and his temple. Such redemption, of course, is part of the total redemption achieved by Jesus.

In chapter 5 we considered the meaning of the Sabbath. The requirement for Israel to refrain from work and to rest on the seventh day of the week harkens back to the creation account that tells of God resting on the seventh day when all his work of creation is finished. Along with circumcision, the sign of God's promises in the covenant, the observance of the Sabbath is a primary mark of covenant obedience. The second giving of the commandments (Deuteronomy 5) links the Sabbath rest with the redemptive work of God in the exodus from Egypt. The redemptive history of the Sabbath can be summarized thus:

- God rests on the seventh day, having created all things in six days
- The Sabbath signifies God's provision for his people in the wilderness
- The Sabbath commandments in Exodus 20 and Deuteronomy 5 are motivated by creation and redemption
- Jesus keeps the Sabbath as a Jew but demonstrates its real meaning
- Paul argues against both Sabbath-keeping and circumcision for Gentile Christians
- Hebrews shows the eschatological significance of the Sabbath and God-given rest.

Life Matters That Are Informed by Biblical Theology

i. Exile and homelessness

Our biblical theology of exile and homelessness has shown us that our natural state is that of living under the judgment of God and being outside the place originally created in which humanity experienced fellowship with God. It is only because of the grace and mercy of God that the universe, and humanity with it, did not immediately end because of the human rebellion recorded in Genesis 3. Genesis 4, with all that follows, provides hope in a fallen world. In hindsight, once the gospel is revealed in Jesus, we can see that the Old Testament promises of God relating to the homecoming of his elect people do not find fulfilment until the coming of Christ.

In the meantime those who, like Abraham, grasped the promises by faith, are deemed by God to have grasped the reality to come. Although they died not having reached the goal in this world, they have been justified by faith; by believing the shadow they are regarded as having grasped the reality in Christ. It is not wrong, therefore, to say that the true believers of the Old Testament were saved by faith in Christ, even though they knew him only by the shadow. The exodus redemption and the entry into the Promised Land do not lead to the fullness of God's kingdom, but they do turn out to be the vital foreshadowing of the future glory. But the coming of the King in his gospel also leaves the people of God to live by faith and not by sight, even though the goal and the means of reaching it are revealed in that gospel.

The New Testament continues to develop, though with a difference, the Old Testament theme of exile and the homelessness of humanity. Christian existence must take this into account. The conviction that a Christian who dies goes 'home to be with the Lord' is sound. Each of us needs to take stock of what kind of hope we have and how it shapes the way we think and live in the present. A mindset of this-worldliness has always been recognized as a major snare for believers. Paul's warning against a 'fleshly' mindset is serious:

> To set the mind on the flesh is death, but to set the mind on the Spirit is life and peace. For the mind that is set on the flesh is hostile to God, for it does not submit to God's law; indeed, it cannot. Those who are in the flesh cannot please God.
>
> *Rom. 8:6–8*

Do not be conformed to this world, but be transformed by the renewal of your mind, that by testing you may discern what is the will of God, what is good and acceptable and perfect.

Rom. 12:2

The transformed mindset is the opposite of that adopted by Adam and Eve when they chose human autonomy and rejected submission to God's word.

Each of us, in our own life-situation, needs to be constantly appraising the extent to which the world shapes our thinking and, thus, our lifestyle. This will never be easy. In the affluent and developed parts of the world, what we class as poverty would rank as untold riches in some countries. This is not the place to try to expand on wealth and poverty. But it is the place to urge that we never allow ourselves to regard the comfort, or otherwise, of the life we lead to be the criterion for assessing our existence. Home is not in this world. Meanwhile, because of the gospel, we persist in works of ministry, in deeds of mercy and compassion, in giving aid to the less fortunate, and in using what wealth we possess to further the spread of the gospel.

Recognition of our ongoing exile and homelessness should motivate all the good works for which God has created us in Christ Jesus (Eph. 2:10). The list is endless but here are a few suggestions:

a. The aspirations of secular humankind for comfort and affluence should be transformed by understanding the needs of a world in darkness and the plight of the multitudes without Christ.
b. Evangelism and deeds of mercy should have a considerable effect in our seeking to defend the defenceless, to feed and house the poor and, above all, to make Christ known.

c. Being exiles in a world that is hostile to God and his gospel means that we will easily arouse hostility and anger in those who espouse non-Christian values. Without fostering a siege mentality in the churches, pastors should preach and teach truthfully about the church in a hostile world.

d. The church should encourage academic rigour in its training of pastors and teachers so that the challenges of the worldly mindsets of our age can be counter-challenged and the integrity of the Christian worldview asserted and maintained. The church needs to be armed against alien philosophies, unbiblical ethical stances, and the constant secular urgings 'to join the twenty-first century'.

ii. The city

Our biblical-theological study of the city was driven by the importance in the biblical story of two cities: Babylon and Jerusalem. We saw that the city began outside the Garden of Eden, built by people in exile. But even in its sinful expressions the city was an attempt to mimic the significance of Eden. In one sense, the buildings and other structures that we regard as the identifying characteristics of any great city are incidental. The real essence is the society of a city; the conglomerate of people seeking to relate meaningfully and safely. In the Old Testament especially, we saw that the cities of Canaan were full of snares for God's people because they were the centres of godless religion and idolatry. In that respect, nothing has changed. We saw how the city came to represent the spiritual state of a people. The fact that the book of Revelation portrays the final home of God's people as the new Jerusalem from heaven indicates that even the most rural-minded, farm-dwelling, city-shy

Christian needs to come to terms with the biblical imagery of the city. We either belong to the city of evil or the city of God; to Babylon or Jerusalem.

The city and the temple are parallel themes. Paul, in 2 Corinthians 6:14–18, appeals to his readers as 'the temple of the living God'. He then links Leviticus 26:12 with Isaiah 52:11.[3] He urges believers to recognize the distinctions between themselves and the world. Some commentators regard the passage in Isaiah as referring to Babylon, others to the cities of Egypt and the exodus. I do not think it much matters which we opt for, since the typologies of the exodus from Egypt and the exodus from Babylon converge; they foreshadow the same thing. The fulfilment they both point to is our redemption in Christ. Paul's application is to the integrity of Christian living as involving an authentic separation from the secular; of light from darkness, and of righteousness from lawlessness:

> What accord has Christ with Belial? Or what portion does a believer share with an unbeliever? What agreement has the temple of God with idols? For we are the temple for the living God; as God said,

> 'I will make my dwelling among them and walk among them,
> > and I will be their God,
> > and they shall be my people.
> Therefore go out from their midst,
> > and be separate from them, says the Lord,

---

[3] Here Paul appears to quote the Old Testament rather freely and there is some dispute over which passages he is quoting. He is possibly quoting here from the Septuagint (Greek) Old Testament.

and touch no unclean thing;
>
> then I will welcome you,
>
> and I will be a father to you,
>
>> and you shall be sons and daughters to me,
>
> says the Lord Almighty.'

2 Cor. 6:15–18

The questions Paul raises in this passage remind us of the importance of seeking to understand how our salvation in Christ works out on the ground. In seeking to live an authentic Christian life, we find that some issues are black and white, and others are more nuanced and require us, with wisdom and within the fellowship of the church, to come, as far as possible, to a godly mind.

As before, I can only make some suggestions regarding our practical applications of the biblical theology we have explored:

a. Idolatry (religion) is the godless and corrupted mimicry of revealed truth about God. People who claim to have no religion usually have a 'religion'; they just do not recognize the nature of their faith. Atheistic evolutionism is a prime example of 'religion-less' religion, a religion of rationalist empiricism, embracing the exercise of implausible faith in time plus chance. It illustrates the way 'religion' functions as a means, not of finding God, but of evading him. The biblical declaration of 'no other name' (Acts 4:12) means that theistic, even monotheistic, religions that do not centre on the redeeming work of Jesus Christ are idolatrous means of avoiding God's revealed truth.

b. Israel's tabernacle, and then the temple, explicitly portrayed both the presence of God and the separation of sinful humanity from God. When Jesus cleansed the temple in

Jerusalem, he not only judged the way the temple had come to be used, but he pointed to himself as the true and holy temple. Now, in Christ, we are built into the temple and should reflect its holiness, individually and as the church.

c. Whatever our preference for lifestyle, we are destined for our rest in the city of God. Be encouraged that none of the evils we associate with cities will exist there. Nor need we suppose that the positive aspects of the city – art, music, technology, relationships and the presence of God – will be limited by our finiteness.

d. Life in this world, overshadowed as it is by the city of evil, will always challenge the Christian with temptations to conform to the ostensibly beneficial aspects of modernity, which are transitory and deceptive.

e. Chief among the snares of the city are ethical modernity and religious syncretism. The Christian church will always be criticized for not keeping up with and adopting the world's changing values. Modern humanism assumes that the latest is always the best and that any attempt to retain yesterday's values must be condemned.

iii. The Sabbath rest

I realize that not all Christians will agree with my take on the Sabbath law and its meaning for us as Christians. For some, Sabbath really does apply to what we do on Sundays. For others, we do on Sundays some Sabbath-like things but not for reasons of legal prescription. There can be little dispute that Jesus saw the growing Pharisaic legalism as a threat to the proper idea of the Sabbath. When we come to Hebrews and its teaching about the Sabbath rest for the people of God, there is an undeniable application of the concept of rest to the final destiny of believers.

I have put forward an understanding of the fulfilment of the Sabbath as a covenant ordinance rather than a universally applicable creation ordinance. I believe that the rationale for Sabbath given in Deuteronomy 5:12–15 demonstrates this clearly by grounding it on Israel's covenant-based salvation from exile in Egypt (Exod. 2:23–25). Furthermore, the Deuteronomic law of Sabbath illustrates the convergence of our main themes in a way that enables us to gather all into the theme of rest as expounded in Hebrews 3 and 4. In asserting the superiority of Christ over Moses, the writer of Hebrews moves on to apply this superiority in the same way that Psalm 95 does. The warnings about failing to enter the rest are applied to the eschatological rest for the people of God. This Sabbath rest (Heb. 4:9), then, embraces the whole range of what the people of God can look forward to.

First, the Sabbath rest for the people of God speaks of a return from our exile and homelessness in a fallen world. In so doing it must also speak of the salvation of the individual from the corruption of sin. Sin is the expression of a radical moral revolt against the Creator and Lord of all. Truly we can look forward to 'going home to be with the Lord'. All the images of the restoration of Eden in the prophets and, finally, in Revelation 22, point to the reality of a form of fellowship with God and his Christ that is not sullied by our fallenness into sin.

Second, the Sabbath rest speaks to us of our citizenship of the new and heavenly Jerusalem which is the centre of the new earth (Rev. 21:1–27). The city and its temple were the focal points of the promised land, the place where God is pleased to dwell with his people. The literalist may see the imagery of a cubed city of over 1,300 miles in each direction as an appalling prospect of the worst of high-rise city congestion. Those more attuned to the apocalyptic and mainstream Old Testament imagery will perhaps recognize the echo of the perfect cube of the Holy of Holies in the temple. For Israel, it had been the forbidden place of God's dwelling where only the mediating high priest could enter with the blood of sacrifice, and that only once a year (Lev. 16). The mercy seat on the ark was guarded by the cherubim just as re-entry into Eden had been. Now the Holy Place is the very dwelling of the people of God in the most intimate presence of God.

Third, the Sabbath rest speaks of itself. That is, it harkens back to the perfection of creation in which God rested from that work and declared it good. The created humans lacked nothing in this world; all was provided as an expression of God's love for them. It harkens back to the saving work of God that he graciously undertook, despite the awful rebellion against him. It speaks of the rest that God's people expressed on one day in seven, by showing that they trusted God to provide for their needs. It speaks of the rest he gave them in the promised land, even though the people themselves spoiled that rest and repudiated it by their idolatry and disobedience. Above all it speaks of the Saviour who came to give rest to all who come to him. This is a rest that is to be believed because it is not empirically obvious while we are strangers in a foreign land at enmity with a fallen world. Thus, it draws us to contemplate our heavenly home, which we already possess in Christ and which will be our real empirical situation for ever when Christ returns in glory.

The practical implications of the Sabbath rest include the following:

a. The sovereignty of God is the foundation of the Sabbath rest. He has done all and has left nothing undone that was needed for human existence, procreation and meaningful relationships. This providential working of God is a reality for Christians today. Hardship and suffering are experienced because of humanity's sinfulness and the enmity of the world towards God and his Christ. Nevertheless, God does not leave us as orphans (John 14:1–20), and he promises to provide for all our needs 'according to his riches in glory' (Phil. 4:19).

b. Israel's Sabbath did provide for everyone, including household servants. We have rightly recognized the human need for physical and mental rest and recreation. But the emphasis in Scripture is not on our personal needs as such, but on the goodness of God in providing for them. We believe in the day off, not for reasons of God's law but because of God's provision for our frailty.

c. The Sabbath teaches us to look forward to the rest that God has in store for us. We can echo Paul's sentiments: 'I consider that the sufferings of this present time are not worth comparing with the glory that is to be revealed to us' (Rom. 8:18). We know that, in Christ, we have already arrived at our goal; and that should be the mainstay and encouragement for us in the face of any struggles of the present.

d. The only way to rightly observe God's Sabbath is by being in Christ, who has already entered that rest (Heb. 4:3). To make Sunday our version of the Jewish Sabbath is to ignore its Christ-centredness, and to return to the law of Moses, something the New Testament constantly warns against. It is to return to the shadow when the substance is Christ (Col. 2:17). It is better by far to retain the name Sabbath for Saturday. Let the Lord's Day be special, holy and observed; but not a Sabbath. By contrast, the true Sabbath rest is a powerful biblical theme for evangelism and a warning against hardness of heart.

e. Entering the Sabbath rest means coming to Christ who gives us rest. We saw in the earlier discussion that the presence of God among his people in the tabernacle and temple was qualified by the need for a priestly ministry. Being near God and having God near to the believer was a mediated matter. A Christian has, in the sense of Hebrews 3 and 4, entered that rest. Christ is our mediator who has entered the presence of the Father. As Hebrews 12:18–24 tells us, coming to Jesus means coming to Zion, the heavenly Jerusalem.

How near do you feel you are to God at any one time? Some will express the feeling of being closer to God when praying, receiving Holy Communion, or reading the Bible. It is important to recognize that how near we are to God, and he to us, does not depend on how near we feel we are, nor on what we are doing. Intermittent feelings of being nearer to God are probably simply a matter of being more focused on the permanent reality. If we are in Christ by faith, we are as close to God, and he to us, as the Son is to the Father and the Father to the Son.

Home to Rest

'A Sabbath rest for the people of God' should be a sweet sound to the believer's ears! As this study has attempted to demonstrate, it is a theme central to the whole biblical drama. Exile, homelessness, the concentration of human evil in the city, and godless idolatry, are all dealt with under the gracious covenant of salvation that God has revealed and fulfilled in Jesus. In dealing with the themes of exile and homelessness, the city, and the Sabbath, and by using a biblical-theological approach, I have tried to show that each provides a way of focusing on the final destiny of all God's people. Each contributes to our understanding of what it means to be at home with the Lord; to rest from our labours; to flee the evil of the godless city; to find rest with God's Christ in the holy city of God, the new Jerusalem from heaven. Thus, we can be encouraged in our quest to live godly lives in an alien world with full confidence in the grace of perseverance and of our final arrival in the place where all the ills caused by human rebellion against God are healed. We can identify with the biblical events and the imagery that point to our salvation in Christ. We can join with the Christian writers who have employed the biblical imagery to describe our pilgrimage to glory. Thus John Bunyan wrote of Mr Valiant for Truth:

> When the day that he must go hence was come, many accompanied him to the River-side, into which as he went he said, *Death, where is thy Sting?* And as he went down deeper he said, *Grave, where is thy Victory?* So he passed over, and all the Trumpets sounded for him on the other side.
>
> *John Bunyan,* Pilgrim's Progress

Index of Scripture References

Index of Subjects and Names

The Goldsworthy Trilogy

Three Classic Books in One Volume:
Gospel and Kingdom
Gospel and Wisdom
The Gospel in Revelation

Graeme Goldsworthy

Hugely popular, this collection is an essential guide for those who seek to understand the whole Bible, in all its unity and diversity, in the light of the gospel of Jesus.

In these three books, the case for a gospel-focused, Christ-centred approach to biblical interpretation is set forth. This method is then applied to both Old Testament Wisdom literature and the New Testament book of Revelation. Goldsworthy argues that both Old and New Testament literature only yield up their true riches when read from the perspective of the gospel.

978-1-84227-036-3

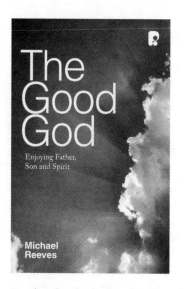

The Good God

Enjoying Father, Son and Spirit

Michael Reeves

In this lively and refreshing book, Michael Reeves unfurls the profound beauty of the Trinity, and shows how the triune God of the Bible brightens everything in a way that is happily life-changing. Prepare to enjoy the Father, Son and Spirit!

'At the heart of the universe is the passionate love between members of the Trinity. Mike Reeves not only helps us grapple with a difficult doctrine but draws us to the magnetically attractive centre of all things. His light touch and theological wisdom combine to provide a truly helpful book which both clears your mind and warms your heart.'

Terry Virgo, Newfrontiers, UK

Michael Reeves is President and Professor of Theology at Union School of Theology.

978-1-84227-744-7

An extract from *The Good God* by Michael Reeves

1.
What was God Doing before Creation?

The dark path and the bright lane

There are two very different ways or approaches to thinking about God. The first way is like a slippery, sloping cliff-top goat-path. On a stormy, moonless night. During an earthquake. It is the path of trying to work God out by our own brainpower. I look around at the world and sense it must have all come from somewhere. Someone or something caused it to be, and that someone I will call God. God, then, is the one who brings everything else into existence, but who is not himself brought into being by anything. He is the uncaused cause. That is *who he is*. God *is*, essentially, The Creator, The One in Charge.

It all sounds very reasonable and unobjectionable, but if I do start there, with that as my basic view of God, I will find every inch of my Christianity covered and wasted by the nastiest toxic fallout. First of all, if God's very identity is to be The Creator, The Ruler, then he needs a creation to rule *in order to be who he is*. For all his cosmic power, then, this God turns out to be pitifully weak: he *needs* us. And yet you'd struggle to find the pity in you, given what he's like. In the aftermath of the Second World War, the twentieth-century Swiss theologian Karl Barth put it starkly:

> Perhaps you recall how, when Hitler used to speak about God, he called Him 'the Almighty'. But it is not 'the Almighty' who is God; we cannot understand from the standpoint of a supreme concept of power, who God is. And the man who calls 'the Almighty' God misses God in the most terrible way. For 'the Almighty' is bad, as 'power in itself' is bad. The 'Almighty' means Chaos, Evil, the Devil. We could not better describe and define the Devil than by trying to think this idea of a self-based, free, sovereign ability.[1]

Now Barth was absolutely not denying that God is Almighty; but he wanted to make very clear that mere might is not who God is.

The problems don't stop there, though: if God's very identity is to be The Ruler, what kind of salvation can he offer me (if he's even prepared to offer such a thing)? If God *is* The Ruler and the problem is that I have broken the rules, the only salvation he can offer is to forgive me and treat me as if I had kept the rules.

But if that is how God is, my relationship with him can be little better than my relationship with any traffic cop (meaning no offence to any readers in the constabulary). Let me put it like this: if, as never happens, some fine copper were to catch me speeding and so breaking the rules, I would be punished; if, as never happens, he failed to spot me or I managed to shake him off after an exciting car chase, I would be relieved. But in neither case would I love him. And even if, like God, he chose

---

[1] Karl Barth, *Dogmatics in Outline* (trans. G. T. Thompson; London: SCM, 1949), p. 48.

to let me off the consequences of my law-breaking, I still would not love him. I might feel grateful, and that gratitude might be deep, but that is not at all the same thing as love. And so it is with the divine policeman: if salvation simply means him letting me off and counting me as a law-abiding citizen, then gratitude (not love) is all I have. In other words, I can never really love the God who is essentially just The Ruler. And that, ironically, means I can never keep the greatest command: to love the Lord my God. Such is the cold and gloomy place to which the dark goat-path takes us.

The other way to think about God is lamp-lit and evenly paved: it is Jesus Christ, the Son of God. It is, in fact, The Way. It is a lane that ends happily in a very different place, with a very different sort of God. How? Well, just the fact that Jesus is 'the Son' really says it all. Being a Son means he has a Father. The God he reveals is, first and foremost, a Father. 'I am the way and the truth and the life', he says. 'No-one comes to the Father except through me' (John 14:6). That is who God has revealed himself to be: not first and foremost Creator or Ruler, but Father.

Perhaps the way to appreciate this best is to ask what God was doing before creation. Now to the followers of the goat-path that is an absurd, impossible question to answer; their wittiest theologians reply with the put-down: 'What was God doing before creation? Making hell for those cheeky enough to ask such questions!' But on the lane it is an easy question to answer. Jesus tells us explicitly in John 17:24. 'Father,' he says, 'you loved me before the creation of the world.' And that is the God revealed by Jesus Christ. Before he ever created, before he ever ruled the world, before anything else, this God was a Father loving his Son.

Athanasius (296?–373)

'He stood for the Trinitarian doctrine'

At the beginning of the fourth century, in Alexandria in the north of Egypt, a theologian named Arius began teaching that the Son was a created being, and not truly God. He did so because he believed that God is the origin and cause of everything, but is not caused to exist by anything else. 'Uncaused' or 'Unoriginate', he therefore held, was the best basic definition of what God is like. But since the Son, being a son, must have *received* his being from the Father, he could not, by Arius' definition, be God.

The argument persuaded many; it did not persuade Arius' brilliant young contemporary, Athanasius. Believing that Arius had started in the wrong place with his basic definition of God, Athanasius dedicated the rest of his life to proving how catastrophic Arius' thinking was for healthy Christian living.

Actually, I've put it much too mildly: Athanasius simply boggled at Arius' presumption. How could he possibly know what God is like other than as he has revealed himself? 'It is,' he said, 'more pious and more accurate to signify God from the Son and call Him Father, than to name Him from His works only and call Him Unoriginate.'[2] That is to say, the right way to think about God is to start with Jesus Christ, the Son of God, not

---

[2] Athanasius, *Against the Arians*, 1.34.

some abstract definition we have made up like 'Uncaused' or 'Unoriginate'. In fact, we should not even set out in our understanding of God by thinking of God primarily as Creator (naming him 'from His works only') – that, as we have seen, would make him dependent on his creation. Our definition of God must be built on the Son who reveals him. And when we do that, starting with the Son, we find that the first thing to say about God is, as it says in the creed, 'We believe in one God, *the Father.*'

That different starting point and basic understanding of God would mean that the gospel Athanasius preached simply felt and tasted very different from the one preached by Arius. Arius would have to pray to 'Unoriginate'. But would 'Unoriginate' listen? Athanasius could pray 'Our Father'. With 'The Unoriginate' we are left scrambling for a dictionary in a philosophy lecture; with a Father things are familial. And if God is a Father, then he must be relational and life-giving, and *that* is the sort of God we could love.

Christ Our Life

Michael Reeves

This wonderful book looks at the person and work of Christ, from his pre-existence and eternal Sonship, through his incarnation, life, death, resurrection and ascension, to his return. It considers and applies the theological significance of all this, looking especially at how all our salvation is found in Christ.

That is, it considers soteriology and the Christian life with and through the lens of Christology. Written in an accessible and devotional manner, with frequent references to historical theologians and their insights, *Christ Our Life* follows on the huge success of the author's best-selling work, *The Good God.*

978-1-84227-758-4

The Genesis of Marriage

God's Declaration, Drama and Purpose

Richard A. Shenk

Marriage seems increasingly irrelevant to many people today. But is this a true understanding of marriage? Could it be that God may have expectations for marriage which are distinct from our own and wholly unaffected by our feelings or debates? If God is the author and definer of marriage, then we must look to the Author to discern its meaning, rather than ourselves.

The Genesis of Marriage sets out a biblical theology of marriage, grounded in the Marriage Text of Genesis 2:18–25, and investigates how it sits in its own context of Genesis 1 – 3 and the whole of Scripture. Doctrinal implications are also explored, answering practical questions such as what are the ethics of marriage? and how do we approach the real-world concerns of separation, divorce and remarriage?

Shenk helps dispel our modern disillusionment with marriage, or at least our ideas and beliefs about marriage which may be at odds with God's, to reveal deep truths about the nature, character and purposes of God.

978-1-78078-994-1

Dangerous Prayer

Discovering a Missional Spirituality in the Lord's Prayer

Darren Cronshaw

Darren Cronshaw shows how the Lord's Prayer offers a radical inspirational framework to help move Christians beyond praying just for themselves and to have their imaginations captured by the mission of God and concern for global needs. *Dangerous Prayer* focuses on principles and stories for training people as prayerful missionaries in their communities. It also offers practical guidance for spiritual, congregational and neighbourhood renewal, fostering not just a 'prayer-life' but a 'life of prayer'.

978-1-84227-976-2

Paternoster:
thinking faith

We trust you enjoyed reading this book
from Paternoster. If you want to be
informed of any new titles from this
author and other releases you can sign
up to the Paternoster newsletter by
scanning below:

Online:
authenticmedia.co.uk/paternoster

Follow us: